RACHAEL RAY 30-MINUTE MEALS
gettogethers

BY RACHAEL RAY

LAKE ISLE PRESS
NEW YORK, NEW YORK

Published by:
Lake Isle Press, Inc.
16 West 32nd Street, Suite 10-B
New York, New York 10001
(212) 273-0796
E-mail: lakeisle@earthlink.net

Distributed to the trade by:
National Book Network (NBN), Inc.
4501 Forbes Boulevard, Suite 200
Lanham, MD 20706
1 (800) 462-6420
http://www.nbnbooks.com

Library of Congress Control Number: 2003112404

ISBN: 1-891105-11-6

Cover photos: Courtesy of The Food Network
Book and cover design: Ellen Swandiak

This book is available at special sales discounts for bulk purchases as premiums or special editions, including personalized covers. For more information, contact the publisher: (212) 273-0796 or by e-mail, lakeisle@earthlink.net

10 9 8 7 6 5 4 3 2 1

DEDICATION

To all the people I get together with—you know who you are. Sharing the love of great food with you has filled my tummy and soul.

SPECIAL THANKS

The list continues to grow, but always at the top, Mamacello a.k.a. my Mom. Mom, you are one little lady with the biggest appetite for life, work, and food, I have ever seen! Without your creative and delicious ideas, and your unwavering support, no one would be reading this book, because it wouldn't exist. I am the luckiest kid, ever!

Another always on the list, Hiroko, my publisher (and my girlfriend, too). I still can't believe what you and your editors do with my ramblings, rants, and recipes with no measurements! You make me look so smart and together on these pages!

Ellen, you are one amazing design team (I say team, because you do the work of 10 people in half the time); you make these pages look so cool! You rock!

Thanks to my Food Network family, especially to Emily on the 30 Minute Meal show. I've taken up residence in your gray matter, Em! We just think alike now. Scary.

My sister, Maria deserves thanks, and she gets my envy, too. When this girl entertains, what a production! She bakes and cooks for days. She produces parties for all ages on a huge scale, and in the end, everything is always perfect and every guest is always happy. Don't people like that annoy you, too? Ria, seriously, you have great GetTogethers (big ones), and I steal ideas from them all the time. You're awesome!

To the rest of my family, I love you all, and I always owe you thanks for your support and ideas.

Boo. I love my dog. She loves food.

John, you are so yummy!

Andy, Andy, and Vicki, you are all very fun to GetTogether with.

Vicky, I love your food and I wish we could GetTogether every night. You're the best!

Alex, Renata, Sabs and Bill, love you all, too.

Anna Maria, it's so nice to share holidays with you! You always have great ideas and delicious recipes, too!

Thanks to fans of the shows and books—you all have GREAT recipe suggestions and your comments and best wishes give me all of my energy! I am so lucky to have the life I have and to work at a job I love. Please, keep me working for years to come!

Thanks, as always, to God. I'm having lots of fun down here!

get togethers

SO—WHAT'S A GET TOGETHER, ANYWAY?

GetTogethers, by my definition, are small, informal gatherings that pair great food with a few great people.

Here's the idea: Instead of throwing 2 or 3 big parties a year, why not invite people in smaller groups and do it more frequently. That way you can select friends, neighbors, or family who are likely to get along and have common interests. They'll enjoy themselves more than they would milling through 50 people in a crowded room. As for you, the host, GetTogethers are decidedly easier, cheaper, and more fun, too! You will actually attend your own gatherings, not just work them. You will be free to spend time with your friends and have real conversations, rather than "hellos" and "goodbyes" sandwiched between bartending and dishwashing.

My advice: Keep things simple, pick a menu and don't overdo it, and most importantly, RELAX.

These days, the only way I entertain is with GetTogethers. And all of them can be prepared in just 30 minutes. Now that's worth raising a glass to!

Cheers!

HELPFUL STORE-BOUGHT ITEMS

Rounding out any party menu is fast and easy when you take advantage of prepared appetizers widely available in today's larger markets.

Meat and Cheese Boards

A large wooden cutting board is a must for cooking because it allows you room to pile ingredients as you process them, without having to transfer each item to a dish or bowl. A cutting board is also the perfect serving platter for one of my favorite starters, a meat and cheese board.

• In the market, near the deli department, you'll find Italian, Spanish, and French sausages in small sizes called "pick-ups." Each usually weighs between 8 and 16 ounces. Buy 2 or 3 in different flavors. Slice or cut half of each sausage into bite-size pieces, leaving the rest whole on the cutting board.

• Select 3 cheeses with the same regional origins as the meats, varying them from a mild to a pungent or blue-veined choice, and serve them with the meats.

Soft Cheeses

Buy goat cheese in logs in 4- or 8-ounce packages. Combine a selection of fresh, chopped herbs: parsley, sage, rosemary, and thyme; or tarragon, chives, parsley, and dill. Using 2 to 3 tablespoons of chopped herbs for a small log, 1/4 cup for a large log, press each end of the log in the herbs to coat. Then roll the log in the remaining herbs. Serve with sliced baguettes or crackers.

Olives

Mix 2 or 3 varieties of gourmet olives found in the bulk bins near your deli counter. Mound the olives in a small serving bowl, and place a ramekin or smaller bowl nearby to collect the pits.

Pâtés

Most markets have selections of individually wrapped pâtés (6- to 8-ounce packages) in both country and mousse styles.

• To serve, garnish the pâté with cracked peppercorns or chopped parsley, and serve with finely chopped red onion, capers, and cornichon or baby gherkin pickles, mini-cocktail rye or pumpernickel slices.

Hummus

Mound hummus in a small bowl topped with crushed red pepper flakes and chopped parsley. Stand flatbreads or bread sticks upright in a tallish hi-ball glass. Fill a second glass with ribs of celery from the heart of the stalk. Place all on a serving plate together.

Garnishes for Plates and Serving Platters

Form small bouquets of any extra herbs and combine them with flower bud arrangements you may have in your home. Arrange and place them around the edges of your serving platters.

• Edible flowers, found in the produce section, also make easy, colorful garnishes.

Nuts

When you place nuts in a bowl, everyone gets their fingers in them, and the nuts end up all over the table. I serve nuts in brandy snifters.

Guests find it easy to pour the nuts out into their hands, without annoying spills.

Chips

Specialty chips of many exotic root vegetables are widely available in larger markets. I love the Terra Chips line of products and often mix several varieties of multi-colored and spiced chips together. Line baskets with napkins to present the chips.
• Corn chips come in many colors and flavors as well. I love to mix red, white, and blue corn tortillas together and serve them in a big, straw sombrero!

Produce

For a relatively small premium, many vegetables are available fresh in ready-to-use packages. We all know and love the sacks of salad greens in every variety, including triple-washed spinach—big timesavers, no doubt!
• Beyond that, look for: trimmed broccoli florets, cauliflower florets, trimmed and washed raw green beans, carrots and celery sticks, bulk-bin artichoke hearts, olives, roasted red peppers, and hot pepper salad. As a 30-minute cook, take help wherever you can find it — and the produce department is an increasingly good place to look for it!

Drinks

I create themes for many of my GetTogethers. When I serve an ethnic menu, I like to provide beverages from that country as well.
• For Asian foods, I serve sakes, Asian beers, and teas.
• For an Italian menu, I'll have San Pelligrino sodas and water on hand, along with Moretti and Peroni beer, red and white table wines, grappa, limoncello, and campari.
• Mexican food calls for margaritas in 2 or 3 flavors, Corona beer and wedges of lime.
• If your friends offer to bring something, suggest some beverages to complement your menu.
• To create an inexpensive ice bucket, line a decorative basket with a clear plastic garbage bag, and fill the basket with ice.
• Serve drinks out of real glasses, not plastic. Mix and match flea market finds. Bar glasses can be had for less than a dollar in discount stores. If they break, it won't break your heart.

Desserts

I'll say it again: I don't bake. So naturally I have an extra set of martini glasses in my cabinet. (I lost you there, I bet.) For easy, elegant desserts, as simple as scooping sorbet, keep a nice set of large martini glasses on hand. Serve ice creams and sorbets in them with a drizzle of liqueur and a fresh fruit garnish, and voilà, dessert!
• Never be afraid to get help from store-bought items for dessert, either. Nothing finishes an Italian menu better than a tray of assorted fresh pastries and cannoli; nothing complements a holiday menu more than warm pie served à la mode.

SETTING THE MOOD

While small gatherings give you more opportunity to visit, they also call greater attention to the details. Here are some helpful suggestions that will make your next GetTogether a really fun event.

Music

Letting your guests help select the music is a cool idea. Encourage your friends to bring their favorite CDs, old or new. Rotate your favorites with theirs. It's the perfect way to bond with guests and to learn about styles of music that you are not familiar with.

Candles

When it comes to lighting, candles are an inexpensive cure-all. Invest in white candles in various sizes, shapes, and heights. Arrange them all around a buffet or dinner table in small groupings. Small pieces of slate from a garden center or flea-market one-of-a-kind dishes make great bases for such "candlescapes."

Setting the Table

Mix and match is the key. When you shop for plates, look into restaurant supply stores and flea markets for real bargains. Try to stick with a particular style—glass, modern, or traditional china. Mix the patterns and colors, but buy a fixed number of plates in different sizes: six 6-inch plates for desserts, six 8-inch plates for dinner, etc.
• Buy boxed sets of plain, tall water glasses and plain tumblers. I use the tall glasses to serve pretzel rods, bread and vegetable sticks. The short glasses are perfect for flat breads, small pretzels, and candies. Juice glasses make terrific bud vases to dot your tables.

Trivets

I serve many casual buffet entrees and warm dips from the pots and dishes in which they were prepared. You'll need trivets; expandable ones to accommodate all sizes of pots and pans can be purchased in restaurant supply stores. They're handy!

Activities

Disposable cameras are a fun party favor because they capture memories-in-the-making. Polaroids are cool, too.

• I set out photo albums of my most recent vacation or special event. I call these albums my *See-Saw* books. I put them on the coffee table so my friends can *see* what I *saw* in my travels.
• For kids at heart, I cover the table with butcher paper and put out baskets of markers and crayons—who doesn't like to doodle?
• Movies are great fun to share with friends. It's a cinch to come up with a theme: pair casual menus with comedy or action films; match more glamorous meals with classics and romance favorites; foreign films inspire ethnic menus.

Last-Minute Fixes

From the garden shed, gather terra cotta pots. When inverted, they make great risers for platters on a buffet. Small pots make terrific holders for flatware.
• Big heavy mirrrors can be taken off the wall, and turned into wonderful serving boards for antipasto or fruit and cheese arrangements.

BRUNCHES
LUNCHES
AND TEA PARTIES, TOO!

Daytime entertaining is fun and affordable, and best of all, kids can attend, too! Breads, eggs, soups, and sandwiches—classic ways to stretch a dollar when feeding a large group—make fabulous, satisfying GetTogether meals. These menus are designed around the celebration of special events: your best friend's or family member's birthday; an intimate baby or bridal shower; or to celebrate a homecoming or personal accomplishment. Relax and enjoy!

RACHAEL RAY 30-MINUTE MEALS
gettogethers

30
MINUTE
MEALS

Various Servings

BRUNCH BEV-IES

1
•

MIX AND MATCH THESE BEVERAGES
WITH ANY BRUNCH MENU:

BLOODY RACHAELS

MAMA-OSAS

JOHN'S MANHATTAN SUNRISE

SUNDAY SCREWDRIVERS

SARATOGA SPRITZ

BLOODY rachaels

1 quart tomato juice or V-8 vegetable juice
8 shots vodka
3 tablespoons prepared horseradish
1 teaspoon coarse black pepper
1 teaspoon celery seed or celery salt (optional)
2 teaspoons Worcestershire sauce
1 tablespoon hot sauce (such as Tabasco)
Juice of 1 lemon
8 stalks celery from the heart with leafy tops
16 jumbo pimiento-stuffed olives
Party picks, 3 to 4 inches long

Mix first 8 ingredients in a pitcher and stir with wooden spoon. Place a stalk of celery into tall glasses. Fill glasses with ice and pour in Bloody Rachael mix. Garnish glasses with 2 jumbo olives on a party pick, balancing ends of pick on rim of glass. Makes 1 pitcher, 8 to 10 servings.

MAMA-osas

This is my mama's twist on a classic, the mimosa. It combines two of her favorite tastes in this life: lemon and champagne. My mother's love of Limoncello, the key ingredient in this drink, is so intense that her nickname has become "Mamacello." Really, it has.

1 shot (1 & 1/2 ounces) Limoncello (lemon-flavored liqueur) (available at larger liquor stores)
4 ounces dry champagne
Lemon zest, for garnish

Frost non-crystal champagne flute in freezer (also a great place to store your Limoncello). Add Limoncello to frosted glass and fill glass with champagne. Garnish with the lemon zest. Makes 1 serving.

John's MANHATTAN SUNRISE

Now, my sweetheart, John, does not do fruity-Sunday-brunch drinks at all. He likes Johnny Walker, Black or Gold, on the rocks. Period. However, Vicki, his mom, loves Manhattans. So, here is a brunch beverage John and I created in honor of Vicki and the city we all love.

1/2 ounce sweet vermouth
1/2 ounce maraschino cherry juice or grenadine
2 shots (3 ounces) scotch whisky
2 ounces orange juice
A splash of soda
Maraschino cherry and sliced orange, for garnish

Pour sweet vermouth and cherry juice into the bottom of a tall glass. Add 4 or 5 ice cubes. Pour in scotch, then orange juice, and top with a splash of soda. Serve with cherry and orange slice for garnish. Makes 1 serving.

sunday SCREWDRIVERS

4 ounces tangerine orange juice, such as Tropicana
1 shot (1 & 1/2 ounces) of citrus vodka
Splash of soda

Pour citrus vodka and tangerine orange juice over ice in a tall glass and top with a splash of soda. Makes 1 serving.

saratoga SPRITZ

1 teaspoon fresh lemon juice plus peel
1 sugar cube
3 dashes bitters
Ginger ale

Put lemon juice, sugar cube, and bitters in a tall glass with ice. Rim edge of glass with lemon curl. Fill with ginger ale. Makes 1 serving.

Serves 6

FARMHOUSE BRUNCH

1
•

HAM AND FONTINA
FRITTATA

2
•

SWISS CHARD WITH
GOLDEN RAISINS

3
•

CORN CAKES WITH
WALNUTS AND SAGE

4
•

SUGARED PEACHES

ham and fontina FRITTATA

1 pound ham steak (from packaged meats case)
1 tablespoon extra-virgin olive oil (evoo) (once around the pan)
2 tablespoons butter
12 extra-large eggs
1/2 cup milk or half-and-half
Salt and freshly ground black pepper, to taste
8 to 10 ounces fontina cheese, shredded (2 cups)

Preheat oven to 400°F.

Trim any connective tissue and all fat off ham steak. Mince the meat into very small bits and set aside.

Heat a 12-inch nonstick skillet with oven-safe handle over moderate heat. (If you only have a rubber-handled skillet, double-wrap the handle in aluminum foil.) Add evoo and 1 tablespoon butter to the skillet and coat sides and bottom of pan evenly with melted butter-and-oil mixture. Add ham bits to the pan and sauté 3 minutes to brown them a bit and cook out some of the moisture in the meat.

Whisk together eggs and milk or half-and-half. Break off tiny pieces of remaining 1 tablespoon butter and drop them into beaten eggs. Season eggs with a little salt and pepper and whisk again to combine. Pour eggs into skillet over ham. Stir eggs gently to evenly distribute bits of ham throughout the eggs. As eggs set, lift up bottom skin that's formed and allow uncooked eggs to settle. Keep doing this as eggs brown until the egg pie begins to set and take form. Transfer to the oven and cook 10 minutes, until golden on top. Add a generous layer of shredded fontina cheese to the frittata and leave in oven another 3 to 5 minutes, or until cheese is melted and begins to bubble and brown. Serve frittata wedges directly from the skillet with a pie server.

> **TIP**
>
> Complete the menu with:
> •
> Assorted sweet rolls
> with jams
> (store-bought)

SWISS CHARD with golden raisins

- 1 & 1/4 to 1 & 1/2 pounds red Swiss chard, stems trimmed
- 1 & 1/2 tablespoons extra-virgin olive oil (evoo) (1 & 1/2 times around the pan)
- 1/8 pound (2 slices) pancetta or bacon, chopped
- 1 small yellow onion, chopped
- 1/4 cup golden raisins (2 handfuls)
- 1 container (14-ounce) chicken broth
- Salt, to taste
- 1/8 teaspoon nutmeg (a couple pinches ground or equivalent of freshly grated)

Heat a large skillet over medium-high heat. Coarsely chop the greens of clean red chard. Add evoo, pancetta, and chopped onion to the pan and cook 2 or 3 minutes, until onions begin to soften and pancetta is lightly browned. Add chopped chard to pan in large bunches, adding remaining chard as the greens wilt. Sprinkle in raisins, pour in broth, and season with salt and nutmeg. Bring liquid to a boil, reduce heat and simmer greens 10 to 15 minutes, until greens are no longer bitter and you are ready to serve. Raisins will plump as the dish cooks through.

CORN CAKES with walnuts and sage

1/4 cup (1/2 stick) butter, plus more for pan and for serving
1 & 1/2 cups water
1 cup cornmeal
2 large eggs
1/2 cup sugar
1/2 cup milk
1 teaspoon salt (1/3 palmful)
1 cup all-purpose flour
4 sprigs fresh sage, slivered (2 tablespoons)
2 ounces walnut halves or pieces (a couple handfuls) (from the bulk bins)
Honey, for serving

Heat a nonstick griddle or nonstick skillet over moderate heat. In a small saucepan, melt butter and transfer to a small mixing bowl. Wipe out pan and return to heat with 1 1/2 cups water. Bring water to a boil over high heat. Add cornmeal to large mixing bowl and scald it with the boiling water; stir to combine. Beat eggs, sugar, and milk with melted butter and stir this mixture into cornmeal. Sprinkle a little salt into bowl. Pour flour into a sieve or a sifter. Knock sieve to add flour into corn cake mix. Add sage to batter and stir to combine.

Wipe a pat of butter nested in paper toweling across the griddle pan to grease it. Place small ladles of corn cake batter onto grill; make cakes 3 inches wide and allow a bit of space between them in the pan. Drop a few walnut bits into wet batter as the cakes begin to cook. Cook cakes 2 to 3 minutes on each side, until golden brown. Serve cakes with softened butter and honey for drizzling. YUMMY!
Makes 12 small corn cakes.

sugared PEACHES

4 or 5 ripe or slightly underripe peaches, pitted and sectioned into wedges
Sugar for sprinkling

Arrange peaches in a spiral on a plate. Sprinkle with sugar and serve.

Serves 6

EASY YET ELEGANT SUNDAY BRUNCH

1

●

ROASTED NEW POTATOES WITH SWEET
PAPRIKA BUTTER AND PARSLEY

2

●

ELSA'S HAM AND
ASPARAGUS TOASTS

3

●

BROILED CITRUS SALAD WITH
COINTREAU, BROWN SUGAR, AND MINT

4

●

SCRAMBLED EGGS
WITH SMOKED SALMON

roasted red NEW POTATOES
with sweet paprika butter and parsley

3 pounds small red new potatoes
1 tablespoon extra-virgin olive oil (evoo)
1/4 cup (1/2 stick) butter
2 teaspoons sweet paprika
1/4 cup parsley leaves, chopped (a couple handfuls)
Salt and freshly ground black pepper, to taste

Preheat oven to 450°F.

Sort potatoes: Those that are 2 inches or less in diameter can be left whole; halve remaining potatoes. Place them in a roasting pan and coat very lightly with a drizzle of evoo. Roast potatoes 20 to 25 minutes, until just tender. Melt butter in a small pan with paprika. Transfer potatoes from the oven to a bowl. Pour melted paprika butter over the potatoes. Sprinkle in parsley and season the potatoes with salt and pepper. Toss the potatoes with paprika butter to coat evenly. Adjust salt and pepper to taste and serve.

elsa's ham and asparagus TOASTS

1 pound thin asparagus spears
Dash of salt, for water
1 loaf chewy, crusty farmhouse-style bread, cut into 1-inch slices
1/4 cup (1/2 stick) butter, softened
2 tablespoons Dijon or grainy mustard
1 & 1/4 pounds boiled, baked, or smoked ham (order thick slices at deli counter)
Freshly ground black pepper, to taste
1 pound fontina cheese, shredded or sliced

TIP

To trim asparagus: Holding an asparagus spear at each end, snap off the tough stem. Use this spear as a guide to trim the bundle with a sharp knife.

Simmer asparagus in salted boiling water, 3 minutes. Drain and reserve cooked spears.

Preheat the broiler.

Toast thick slices of bread under broiler, 6 inches from heat. Combine softened butter and mustard. Spread the toasted bread with mustard butter. Cut sliced ham into smaller pieces to process. Grind the ham in a food processor. Spread the toast with ground ham. Arrange steamed asparagus spears on top of the ham. Top each toast with a few grinds of black pepper and a mound of fontina cheese. Return toasts to hot oven under broiler and cook until cheese melts and lightly browns at edges. Arrange on a platter and serve.

broiled CITRUS SALAD
with cointreau, brown sugar, and mint

2 quarts of jarred citrus salad, **drained**
3 ounces Cointreau **or other orange liqueur**
1/3 cup brown sugar **(3 handfuls)**
Several sprigs fresh mint, **torn or chopped, for garnish**

Preheat the broiler to high.

Arrange drained citrus in a casserole dish. Douse fruit with liqueur. Top fruit with 3 handfuls of brown sugar sprinkled evenly over the top. Place casserole under hot broiler 6 inches from heat for 7 or 8 minutes, until sugar just begins to brown and bubble. Garnish warm casserole with torn or chopped fresh mint leaves and serve.

BRUNCHES LUNCHES AND TEA PARTIES...TOO!

SCRAMBLED EGGS with smoked salmon

1/4 pound sliced smoked salmon
12 eggs
1/2 cup heavy cream
12 to 15 blades of fresh chives, **finely chopped**
Salt **and freshly ground black** pepper, **to taste**
2 tablespoons butter

Reserve 2 slices of salmon for garnish; chop the remaining salmon into very small pieces. Whisk eggs and cream together. Add half of the chopped chives and season eggs with salt and pepper. Preheat a large nonstick skillet over medium heat. Melt butter in the pan and add eggs. Scramble eggs with a wooden spoon, taking care not to cook them dry. When eggs have come together but remain wet, stir in chopped salmon. Remove pan from the stove and place on a trivet. Garnish the eggs with remaining salmon and chives and serve right out of the warm pan.

TIP

If you are serving these eggs with the other recipes provided as a brunch, a platter of store-bought fruit-filled Danish pastries will complete your elegant brunch. Allow one Danish per person but halve them so that guests may mix and match varieties.

MENU

Serves 6

CARB-BUSTING BRUNCH

1

CUCUMBER SNACKERS

2

BLT FRITTATA

3

STRAWBERRIES AND CREAM
WITH MACADAMIA NUTS

CUCUMBER snackers

You'll never miss that cracker!

1/3 to 1/2 English (seedless) cucumbers, **cut into eighteen 1/4-inch slices**
2 or 3 pinches salt
6 ounces herb cheese **(such as Boursin)**
1/4 pound smoked Norwegian salmon, **thinly sliced**
Freshly ground black pepper, **to taste**

Set cucumber slices on paper towels to drain and dry. Season lightly with salt. Spread each slice of cucumber with a little cheese. Arrange cucumbers on a serving plate. Top each snacker with a small piece of salmon. Crack a little black pepper over the snackers and serve or chill until ready to serve Makes 18 pieces.

BLT frittata

3 tablespoons extra-virgin olive oil (evoo) (3 times around the pan)
1/4 pound sliced pancetta, chopped
4 cloves garlic, chopped
2 bundles arugula, trimmed and chopped (about 3 loosely packed cups)
1 can (15 ounces) diced tomatoes, drained
12 extra-large eggs
1/3 cup half-and-half (eyeball it)
1 teaspoon salt
Freshly ground black pepper, to taste

Preheat oven to 400°F.

Heat a 12-inch nonstick skillet over medium-high heat. Use a pan with an oven-safe handle or wrap the handle with 2 layers of aluminum foil. Add evoo and pancetta to the pan. When pancetta browns at edges and begins to crisp, add garlic and arugula. Wilt arugula; stir in tomatoes. Beat eggs together with half-and-half. Add salt and pepper and whisk in seasoning. Pour eggs over arugula and let eggs set. Using a spatula, raise eggs off the bottom of the skillet to allow more of the liquid egg to settle. When the frittata has set, transfer to oven and cook 10 to 12 minutes until top is deep golden brown. Remove the frittata and let it stand 5 minutes. Cut into wedges and serve.

STRAWBERRIES and CREAM
with macadamia nuts

2 pints strawberries, hulled and halved or quartered
1 cup whipping cream
1 rounded tablespoon sugar
1 cup macadamia nuts, chopped

Pile strawberries into 6 small dessert cups or glass dishes. Beat cream and sugar into soft peaks. Pile cream on top of berries and sprinkle chopped macadamia nuts on top.

Serves 2

BREAKFAST IN BED FOR A KING AND A QUEEN

1
●

PAIN PERDU
(LOST BREAD, A.K.A. FRENCH TOAST)

2
●

THREE-BERRY COMPOTE

3
●

HOMEMADE MAPLE FENNEL SAUSAGE PATTIES

PAIN PERDU (lost bread, a.k.a. french toast)

2 eggs

1 cup sugar

1 tablespoon cornstarch, **dissolved in a splash of water**

1 cup whole milk

1/2 teaspoon nutmeg

6 slices stale white bread

Butter, **for pan**

TIP

Other suggested
toppings:

•

Warm maple syrup
and butter

•

Powdered sugar

•

Cinnamon sugar

•

Fresh berries and
whipped cream

Preheat a nonstick griddle or skillet over medium heat. Beat eggs very well, add sugar and beat again. Add cornstarch in water and beat that in, then beat in milk and nutmeg. Coat bread thoroughly with egg mixture. Lightly butter hot pan with butter nested in paper towel. Add bread to the pan and cook slowly, 3 or 4 minutes on each side, 2 to 3 slices at a time. Serve hot with your favorite toppings or Three-Berry Compote.

homemade maple fennel
SAUSAGE PATTIES

1/2 teaspoon coarse salt
1/2 teaspoon coarse black pepper
1 teaspoon fennel seeds
2/3 pound ground pork
2 tablespoons maple syrup
1 tablespoon olive oil or vegetable oil

Combine salt, pepper, and fennel in the bottom of a bowl. Add pork and mix to combine with spices. Pour maple syrup over the pork and work the meat again to combine. Form meat into patties, 3 inches around. Heat a nonstick skillet over medium-high heat. Add 1 tablespoon oil and cook patties 4 minutes on each side. Drain on a paper towel-lined plate, then serve. Makes 6 patties.

THREE-BERRY compote

1/3 cup sugar (eyeball it)
2 teaspoons lemon juice (juice of 1/4 lemon)
1/3 cup water (eyeball it)
1/2 pint strawberries, sliced
1/2 cup raspberries
1/2 cup blackberries
1/4 cup maple syrup or honey

Combine sugar, lemon juice, and water in a small saucepan. Over moderate heat, dissolve sugar into water. Stir in fruit, coating it in sugar-water, and bring the fruit and water to a bubble. Reduce heat and simmer, 5 minutes. Remove fruit with a slotted spoon to a serving dish and add maple syrup or honey to the pan. Thicken syrup 5 minutes and pour over fruit. Serve with French toast (see recipe), pancakes, or waffles.

Serves 8

SOUTHERN COMFORTS BRUNCH

1

SPIRAL-SLICED HAM WITH JEZEBEL
SAUCE AND CHEESE BISCUITS

2

BRAISED MUSTARD GREENS

3

FRIED GREEN TOMATOES

4

MASHED SWEET POTATOES

spiral-sliced HAM with jezebel sauce and CHEESE BISCUITS

Ham and Sauce

1 spiral-sliced cooked ham

1 can (15 ounces) crushed pineapple

1 jar (10 ounces) apricot all-fruit preserves

3 tablespoons dry mustard

1/2 cup prepared horseradish (from dairy aisle)

1 teaspoon black pepper

Biscuits

2 boxes (10 to 12 ounces each) biscuit mix (such as Jiffy brand), mixed to package directions

1 cup shredded cheddar cheese

1/4 teaspoon ground or freshly grated nutmeg (a couple pinches)

Preheat oven to 425°F.

Remove ham from packaging and cover loosely in aluminum foil. Bake to warm ham through, 25 to 30 minutes.

Make the sauce: Combine remaining ingredients in a bowl.

Make the biscuits: Combine prepared biscuit mix with cheddar cheese and nutmeg. Bake biscuits on a nonstick cookie sheet according to package directions. Makes 16 biscuits. Serve with warmed ham and sauce.

braised MUSTARD GREENS

4 slices bacon, **chopped**
2 pounds mustard greens, **trimmed and chopped**
2 tablespoons white vinegar
2 teaspoons sugar
Coarse salt, **to taste**
2 cups chicken broth

In a large skillet over medium-high heat, brown bacon and render the fat. Add chopped greens to the pan in bunches and turn until they wilt, then add more greens. When all of the greens are in the pan, add vinegar and cook a minute. Season greens with sugar and salt. Add chicken broth to the pan and cover. Reduce heat to medium-low and simmer greens 15 to 20 minutes, then serve.

fried GREEN TOMATOES

1 cup all-purpose flour
2 eggs, **beaten**
1/4 cup milk
1 cup cornmeal
1 teaspoon curry powder **(eyeball it)**
1 teaspoon sweet paprika
1 teaspoon salt
1/4 teaspoon cayenne pepper
6 green tomatoes, **sliced**
3 to 4 tablespoons vegetable oil **(4 times around the pan)**
1/2 cup chili sauce
1/2 cup sour cream

Preheat skillet over medium-high heat. Place 1/2 cup flour in a pie plate. Beat eggs and milk together in a second pie plate or shallow dish. Combine the remaining 1/2 cup flour, the cornmeal, and spices in a third shallow dish. Coat sliced tomatoes in flour, egg, and seasoned cornmeal. Add 2 tablespoons (twice around the pan) vegetable oil to the hot skillet and fry half of the tomato slices 2 to 3 minutes on each side; repeat. Serve hot with chili sauce mixed with sour cream or your favorite condiment. Makes 24 slices.

BRUNCHES LUNCHES AND TEA PARTIES, TOO!

mashed SWEET POTATOES

3 pounds sweet potatoes, **peeled and cut into chunks**
1/2 stick butter
1/2 banana, **sliced**
Zest and juice of 1 orange
1 cup chicken broth
1/2 cup brown sugar
1/2 teaspoon nutmeg
Salt **and freshly ground black** pepper, **to taste**

Boil potatoes until tender and drain. Return the pot to the stovetop over medium heat. Add butter and bananas to the pot. Cook bananas 5 minutes and add the juice of 1 orange to the pot; reserve the zest. Allow the juice to cook out, 1 minute. Add potatoes to the pot and the broth and sugar. Mash potatoes, banana, broth, and sugar together until well combined. Season with nutmeg, salt, pepper, and orange zest to taste. Mash to combine spices and serve.

LITE BITES PARTY

NEW YEAR'S EVE SUPPER

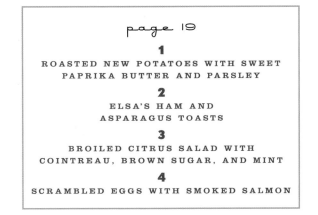

EASY YET ELEGANT
SUNDAY BRUNCH

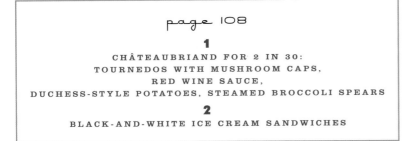
MEAT AND POTATOES À DEUX

BIG WRAP TAILGATE PARTY

A GET AWAY FOR ANY DAY BAJA BLOWOUT

SNACK ATTACK PARTY

30 MINUTE MEALS

MENU

Serves 8

TEX-MEX BRUNCH

1

BEEF AND BLACK BEAN CHILI
AND CORN-CHIP CASSEROLE

2

ROASTED RED PEPPER
AND POTATO EGG PIE

3

MEXICAN SALAD
WITH TOMATOES, ONIONS, AND
AVOCADO DRESSING

beef and black bean CHILI and CORN-CHIP CASSEROLE

2 pounds 90% lean ground beef sirloin

1 tablespoon extra-virgin olive oil (evoo) (once around the pan)

Salt and freshly ground black pepper, to taste

1 tablespoon Worcestershire sauce (eyeball it)

1 medium onion, finely chopped

4 to 6 cloves garlic, finely chopped

1 can (6 ounces) sliced jalapeño peppers

2 & 1/2 to 3 tablespoons dark chili powder (2 palmfuls)

1 tablespoon cumin

1 cup beef stock or broth

1 can (14 ounces) diced stewed tomatoes

1 can (8 ounces) tomato sauce

2 cans (15 ounces each) black beans, drained

3 cups corn chips (such as Frito brand)

2 cups shredded Monterey Jack or cheddar cheese

2 tablespoons chopped fresh cilantro (a handful) (optional)

3 scallions, chopped

In a large, deep skillet or pot, brown ground beef in evoo over high heat. Season meat with salt and pepper, then add Worcestershire sauce. When the meat is browned and crumbled, reduce heat to medium-high then add onion, garlic, and jalapeño. Season veggies and meat with chili powder and cumin. Cook veggies and meat together 5 minutes. Stir in broth and scrape up pan drippings. Stir in diced tomatoes, tomato sauce, and black beans. When the mixture comes to a bubble, reduce heat and simmer 5 minutes more.

Preheat broiler.

Transfer chili to a shallow casserole and top with corn chips and cheese. Melt cheese under broiler. Top casserole with cilantro and scallions; serve.

roasted red pepper and potato EGG PIE

- 1/2 cup extra-virgin olive oil (evoo) (eyeball it)
- 2 medium Russet potatoes, peeled and halved, then thinly sliced across into half-moons
- 1 small onion, halved, then very thinly sliced
- 2 roasted red peppers (jarred or from bulk bins of market), drained and sliced
- 10 large eggs, beaten
- Salt and freshly ground black pepper, to taste

Heat about 1/4 cup evoo in a 10- to 12-inch nonstick skillet with an oven-proof handle over medium-high heat. Add sliced potatoes and fry in evoo until they begin to become tender, 5 minutes. Add onions and cook 5 minutes more. Remove potatoes and onions to a bowl using a slotted spoon. Wipe out pan, return pan to heat and add remaining evoo. Reduce heat under pan to medium.

Place a rack 6 inches from the broiler in oven. Preheat broiler to high.

Add sliced roasted red peppers to potatoes and onions. Season beaten eggs with salt and pepper and add to cooked vegetables. Add mixture to the pan and cook until eggs settle and brown on the bottom. Transfer pan to broiler and allow the egg pie to brown on top and puff up.

Slide tortilla (egg pie) out of the pan and onto a large serving plate. Cool slightly, then cut into 8 wedges and serve.

BRUNCHES LUNCHES AND TEA PARTIES, TOO!

MEXICAN SALAD
with tomatoes, red onions and, avocado dressing

Salad

2 heads Bibb lettuce, cleaned and dried

4 medium red vine-ripe tomatoes, cut into wedges

2 medium yellow vine-ripe tomatoes, cut into wedges

1/2 large red onion, thinly sliced

Dressing

2 ripe avocados

Juice of 1 lemon

1 small jalapeño pepper, seeded and chopped

3 tablespoons chopped red onion (steal it from your salad)

2 tablespoons fresh cilantro leaves (a handful)

1 teaspoon coarse salt

3 tablespoons water (a couple splashes)

3 tablespoons extra-virgin olive oil (evoo)

Build your salad on a large platter: Use Bibb lettuce as the bed, then layer the tomatoes and scatter the red onions around the platter.

Make the dressing: Cut avocados in half lengthwise, cutting around the pit. Separate the halves and scoop out the pits with a spoon, then use the spoon to scoop the avocados from their skins. Place the avocados in a food processor bowl and combine with lemon juice, jalapeño, red onion, cilantro, salt, and water. Grind until the avocado mixture is smooth, then stream evoo into dressing. Adjust seasonings and pour over salad, then serve. Dressing may be stored 3 or 4 days in an airtight container.

30 MINUTE MEALS

MENU

Serves 6

A HEARTY LUNCH

1
•

CAULIFLOWER SOUP WITH GARLIC AND CHEESE SOURDOUGH "DIPPERS"

2
•

WILD MUSHROOM AND LEEK FRITTATA

CAULIFLOWER SOUP
with garlic and cheese sourdough "DIPPERS"

Soup

Coarse salt and pepper, to taste

2 heads cauliflower, cut into small bunches of florets

1 tablespoon extra-virgin olive oil (evoo)

2 tablespoons butter

3 stalks celery and leafy tops from the heart of stalk, finely chopped

1 medium onion, chopped

2 tablespoons chopped fresh thyme leaves

2 tablespoons all-purpose flour

1 quart chicken stock or broth

1 cup half-and-half or whole milk

3 tablespoons chopped fresh flat-leaf parsley or chives, for garnish

1/2 cup grated Parmesan cheese for passing at the table

Dippers

3 sandwich-size sourdough English muffins (such as Thomas's brand), split

3 tablespoons butter

1 clove garlic, cracked away from skin

1 cup shredded sharp cheddar cheese

1/2 cup grated Parmesan cheese

1/4 teaspoon sweet paprika

Make the soup: Bring 2 inches water to a boil in a soup pot. Season water with a little salt and add cauliflower. Boil, covered, 10 minutes. Drain cauliflower and transfer to a bowl. Mash with a fork. Return pot to the stovetop over medium heat. Add evoo and butter. When butter has melted into evoo, add celery, onion, and thyme. Sauté veggies 5 minutes, add flour and cook 1 minute more. Whisk in stock, then half-and-half or milk. Raise heat to bring liquid to a boil. Add mashed cauliflower and season with salt and pepper, to taste. Garnish soup with chopped parsley or chives and serve with grated cheese to sprinkle on top.

Preheat broiler.

Make the "dippers": Toast English muffin halves and place on a cookie sheet. In a small sauce pan, melt butter with garlic over low heat. Brush toasted muffins with garlic butter and top with lots of grated cheddar and Parmesan cheeses. Sprinkle a little paprika over toasts, then melt and brown cheeses under broiler, then serve cheesy toasts with soup for dipping.

wild mushroom and leek FRITTATA

2 leeks, trimmed of rough tops (leave 3 to 4 inches of green on white of leek)
2 tablespoons extra-virgin olive oil (evoo) (twice around the pan)
12 crimini mushrooms, sliced
1 cup shiitake mushrooms (a couple handfuls), stems removed, chopped
1 cup oyster mushrooms (a couple handfuls), chopped
Salt and freshly ground black pepper, to taste
Zest of 1 lemon
12 eggs
1/2 cup grated Parmesan cheese

Cut leeks down the center, set flat, then slice into 1/2-inch pieces. Rinse in a colander, separating the layers of the leeks, to remove all of the grit. Dry the sliced leeks by spreading the pieces out on paper towels.

Preheat oven to 400°F.

Heat a 10-inch nonstick skillet with an oven-safe handle over medium to medium-high heat. (Wrapping a rubber handle in foil will allow the pan to transfer to oven as well.)

To hot pan, add evoo and mushrooms. Season mushrooms with salt and pepper. Cook 3 minutes, add leeks, cook 3 to 5 minutes more, until all of the veggies are tender. Sprinkle with lemon zest. Beat eggs with salt and pepper. Pour over the mushrooms and leeks. Lift and settle eggs in the pan as they brown on the bottom. When the eggs are set but remain uncooked on top, transfer to oven for 7 or 8 minutes, until frittata is golden brown and puffy. Sprinkle the frittata with cheese the last minute or two in the oven.

Serve frittata from the hot pan, cutting it into 6 wedges at the table.

30 MINUTE MEALS

MENU

Serves 4

GOTHAM BISTRO LUNCH

1
●

TUNA BURGERS WITH GINGER AND SOY

2
●

GRILLED RED ONIONS

3
●

CRISPY NOODLE SALAD WITH SWEET AND SOUR DRESSING

TUNA BURGERS with ginger and soy

1 & 1/2 pounds fresh tuna steak

2 cloves garlic, chopped

2 inches fresh gingerroot, minced or grated

3 tablespoons Tamari (dark soy sauce)

2 scallions, chopped

1/2 small red bell pepper, finely chopped

2 teaspoons sesame oil

2 teaspoons grill seasoning, such as Montreal by McCormick, or
   1 teaspoon freshly ground black pepper, and 1/2 teaspoon of salt

1 tablespoon light-colored oil, such as safflower, canola, or peanut

1/2 pound shiitake mushrooms, coarsely chopped

Coarse salt, to taste

4 sesame Kaiser rolls, split

1 jar (8 ounces) mango chutney

4 leaves red leaf lettuce

1 jar (8 ounces) wasabi mustard (such as Stonewall Kitchen Brand), or
   Asian sweet hot mustard

Exotic root vegetable chips (such as Terra brand) to pass at table

Pickled ginger, for garnish (optional)

Preheat a nonstick griddle or a grill pan to medium-high to high heat. Cube tuna into bite-size pieces and place in a food processor. Pulse the processor to grind the tuna until it has the consistency of ground beef. Transfer to a bowl. Combine ground tuna with garlic, ginger, soy sauce, scallions, red bell pepper, sesame oil, and black pepper. Form 4 large patties, 1 & 1/2 inches thick. Drizzle patties on both sides with oil.

Cook tuna burgers 2 to 3 minutes on each side for rare, up to 6 minutes each side for well done.

In a medium nonstick skillet over medium-high heat, sauté fresh shiitakes for 2 or 3 minutes in 1 tablespoon oil (once around the pan in a slow stream). Season mushrooms with salt and pepper.

Open up the rolls and lightly toast them under broiler. Spread mango chutney on the bottom of each bun. Top with tuna burger, shiitakes, and lettuce. Spread wasabi mustard or sweet hot mustard on bun tops and set them in place. Serve with exotic chips and pickled ginger, if desired.

grilled RED ONIONS

1 large red onion, unpeeled

Light-colored oil such as peanut, vegetable, or canola, for drizzling

Steak seasoning blend, such as Montreal Seasoning by McCormick, or coarse salt and freshly ground black pepper, to taste

Preheat a grill or nonstick griddle to hot. Trim a thin slice off the side of the whole, unpeeled onion. Set the onion flat on the cut surface for stability. Cut the onion into 4 one-inch-thick slices. Remove the outer ring of skin from each slice. Drizzle the sliced onion with light-colored oil and season both sides with steak seasoning or salt and pepper. Grill on hot grill or on a nonstick griddle for 5 to 7 minutes on each side, until onion is tender and has begun to caramelize.

CRISPY NOODLE SALAD

with sweet and sour dressing

1 sack (6 cups) mixed baby greens

1 cup fresh bean spouts

1 cup shredded carrots (available preshredded in produce department)

4 radishes, sliced

2 scallions, chopped

1/2 red bell pepper, cut into thin strips

2 cups fried noodles, any size (available in bulk bins or on Asian foods aisle of market)

1/4 cup plum sauce (hoisin) or duck sauce

2 tablespoons rice wine vinegar, or cider or white vinegar may be substituted

1/3 cup light-colored oil such as peanut, canola, or vegetable (eyeball it)

Salt and freshly ground black pepper, to taste

In a bowl, combine greens, bean sprouts, carrots, radishes, scallions, red bell pepper, and half of the fried noodles. Whisk together plum or duck sauce and vinegar in a smaller bowl. Stream in oil and continue whisking to combine. Dress salad and toss with salt and pepper, to taste. Serve with remaining crispy noodles as garnish.

Serves 4

BACKYARD BISTRO LUNCHEON

1
•

SALAD LYONNAISE

2
•

LEEK AND POTATO SOUP
WITH GARLIC CROÛTES

3
•

CASSIS-SPLASHED MELON
WITH FRENCH VANILLA ICE CREAM
AND BLACKBERRIES

SALAD LYONNAISE and
leek and potato SOUP with garlic croûtes

3 leeks, trimmed of tough tops (leave 3 to 4 inches of green on white of leek)

1/3 cup plus 2 tablespoons extra-virgin olive oil (evoo), for salad dressing plus more for drizzling

1 bay leaf, fresh or dried

Salt and freshly ground black pepper, to taste

4 all-purpose potatoes (such as Russet), peeled

Salt and freshly ground black pepper

6 cups chicken broth

4 one-inch-thick slices whole-grain French bread

1/3 pound slab bacon (one 1/2-inch slice) (from butcher counter)

1 medium onion, chopped

2 large cloves garlic, cracked away from skin

2 tablespoons white wine vinegar

1 teaspoon Dijon mustard

A few sprigs fresh tarragon, leaves chopped (2 tablespoons)

1 sack prewashed mixed baby greens

1 heart of romaine lettuce, chopped

4 large eggs

A splash of vinegar, any type

1/4 cup shredded Gruyère cheese

Cut leeks in half lengthwise and slice into 1/2-inch pieces. Place in a colander. Separate sliced leeks under cold running water and clean them. Drain.

Preheat oven to 300°F.

Heat a medium soup pot over medium-high heat. Add 2 tablespoons evoo, bay leaf, and leeks. Season with salt and pepper. Slice potatoes thinly, adding them to soup pot as you go. Season potatoes with salt; add chicken broth. Cover soup and bring to a boil. Uncover and simmer 12 to 15 minutes, until potatoes are very tender. Break up potatoes to slightly thicken soup. Remove bay leaf.

While soup simmers, make the croûtes: Place sliced bread in oven directly on rack and toast 5 or 6 minutes, until evenly golden. Meanwhile, cut slab bacon into 1/4-inch slices, making fat matchstick shapes, or batons. Cook bacon in a small nonstick pan over medium-high heat. Remove rendered bacon to paper towels. Return pan to heat and cook chopped onions in bacon drippings over medium heat, 3 to 5 minutes, until just tender.

When toasts come out of oven, rub them liberally with cracked cloves of garlic and drizzle with evoo.

Assemble the salad: Combine vinegar, mustard, and tarragon in a small bowl and whisk in 1/3 cup evoo in a slow stream. Season with salt and pepper and whisk again to combine. Toss mixed baby greens and romaine with dressing and divide greens among 4 plates. Top salads evenly with bacon and onion.

Poach eggs: Bring 2 inches water and a splash of vinegar to a boil, then reduce heat to a low simmer. Crack an egg into a small dish then gently slide the egg into simmering water using the dish to cushion the transfer. Repeat with remaining eggs. Poach eggs 3 minutes, then, using a slotted spoon, transfer eggs to the salads, 1 egg on each salad.

To serve soup, place a croûte in the bottom of each soup bowl. Top each toast with a tablespoon of grated Gruyère cheese. Ladle soup over the croûtes and serve with salads.

cassis-splashed MELON
with french vanilla ice cream and blackberries

1 ripe cantaloupe, **quartered and seeded**
1/2 cup cassis **liqueur or syrup**
1 pint French vanilla ice cream
1/2 pint blackberries

Cut a sliver off the bottom of each melon wedge so that it will sit evenly on dessert plate. Pour 2 tablespoons of cassis liqueur or syrup across each melon wedge. Soften ice cream in microwave on high for 10 seconds. Scoop 1 ball of ice cream onto each wedge of melon. Garnish with a few blackberries and serve.

BRUNCHES LUNCHES AND TEA PARTIES, TOO!

45

Serves 6

BACKYARD LUAU PICNIC

1
•

HONEY TERIYAKI CHICKEN
WITH RIPE PINEAPPLE SPEARS AND
BLACK-AND-WHITE RICE BALLS

2
•

LAVA FLOWS
(OR PIÑA COLADAS WITH RIVERS OF
STRAWBERRY)

3
•

MACADAMIA COCONUT
COOKIE BARS

macadamia coconut COOKIE BARS

1 package dry sugar cookie mix, **mixed to package directions**
1 cup macadamia nuts
1 cup shredded coconut
1 cup white chocolate chips
Softened butter, **for pan**

Preheat oven to 375°F.

To cookie mix prepared to package directions, add nuts, coconut, and white chocolate
chips. Butter a 9x12 baking pan and spread cookie dough evenly in a thin layer
across the baking dish. Bake bars 20 to 22 minutes, or until light golden brown.
Remove from oven, cut into squares, and serve.

honey teriyaki CHICKEN with ripe pineapple spears and black-and-white RICE BALLS

3 cups water

2 tablespoons butter

1 teaspoon salt (eyeball it)

1 & 2/3 cups white rice

3 tablespoons black sesame seeds, or toasted white sesame seeds may be substituted

6 boneless, skinless chicken breasts (6 ounces each)

6 boneless, skinless chicken thighs (4 or 5 ounces each)

Vegetable oil, for drizzling

Coarse salt and coarse black pepper, to taste

1 cup chicken broth

1 inch gingerroot, peeled

1/3 cup honey (eyeball it)

1/3 cup teriyaki sauce

1 tablespoon toasted sesame oil

4 scallions, thinly sliced

1 ripe pineapple

Preheat a grill pan or large griddle over medium-high heat.

Make the rice balls: Bring water to a boil in a medium covered pot. Add butter, salt, and rice to the pot. Return the water to a boil. Reduce heat to simmer and replace cover. Simmer 18 minutes and remove rice from heat. Take the lid off the pot to cool rice a bit. Scoop rice into balls with an ice cream scoop and your hands. Dampen hands with water to work with rice if it is very sticky. Set rice balls on a plate and sprinkle with black sesame seeds.

While the rice is cooking, make the chicken: Lightly coat breasts and thighs with oil, salt, and pepper. Place chicken on hot grill and cook 6 minutes on the first side.

While chicken is cooking, make the sauce: Bring chicken broth and ginger to a boil. Stir in honey. When honey has dissolved into broth, add teriyaki sauce and sesame oil and reduce heat to simmer.

Turn chicken and coat liberally with honey teriyaki sauce using a basting brush. Cook chicken 4 minutes, turn again and baste liberally again with sauce, then cook 2 minutes longer. Remove chicken to a plate. Garnish chicken with sliced scallions.

While chicken cooks on the second side, cut the pineapple: First, cut off top and bottom. Set upright and trim away skin in strips from top to bottom. Halve lengthwise and quarter each half lengthwise, for a total of 8 spears. The core is edible, but tough; it may be trimmed if you wish. Pineapple can be very acidic—spears set in cold water for just 1 minute will keep the fruit from stinging your lips when you eat it. Serve pineapple with chicken and rice balls. This entrée can be served hot or not.

LAVA FLOWS
(or piña coladas with rivers of strawberry)

These can be made as mocktails for the kids (just omit the liquor and add extra ice).

3 cups frozen sliced strawberries in juice, defrosted
2 cans coconut milk drink mix (such as Coco Lopez)
3 cups pineapple juice
6 shots coconut rum or light rum
1 tray of ice cubes

TIP

The recipe calls for defrosted frozen sliced strawberries. When you bring them home from the market, place them on a dish in the refrigerator so they will be soft and ready to process. The dish will catch any leaks or moisture from defrosting.

Blend strawberries in a blender on high speed until smooth. Place 1/2 cup strawberry purée in the bottom of 6 hurricane or double rocks cocktail glasses. Rinse blender and return to base. Place remaining ingredients in blender and blend on high until smooth. Pour piña coladas into glasses on top of the strawberry purée. The purée will run up through the piña coladas, creating a lava flow effect.

BRUNCHES LUNCHES AND TEA PARTIES,TOO!

49

30 MINUTE MEALS

MENU

Serves 4

A LUNCH OF MY FAVORITES

1
•

TOMATO AND SPINACH SOUP

2
•

OVEN FRIES WITH
HERBES DE PROVENCE

3
•

RACHAEL'S TUNA PAN BAGNAT

This tasty lunch also makes a picture-perfect picnic. To take this menu on the road, pour the soup into a large thermos and rather than making the oven fries, buy a sack of specialty potato chips instead. Garlic-and-onion flavored Terra brand chips, available on the snack aisle of your market, are a good example.

OVEN FRIES with herbes de provence

3 all-purpose potatoes, scrubbed and dried
Extra-virgin olive oil (evoo), for drizzling (about 2 tablespoons)
1 tablespoon plus 1 teaspoon dried herbes de Provence (2 palmfuls), or 1 teaspoon each: dried parsley, sage, rosemary, and thyme
Salt, to taste

Preheat the oven to 500°F.
Cut potatoes into thin wedges and place on a cookie sheet. Coat potatoes in a thin layer of evoo, then sprinkle very liberally with 2 palmfuls of herbes de Provence. Toss potatoes to coat evenly. Roast potatoes 25 minutes, until crisp and golden at edges. Season hot wedges with salt.

tomato and spinach SOUP

2 tablespoons extra-virgin olive oil (evoo) (twice around the pan)
1 large shallot, finely chopped
2 cloves garlic, chopped
1 can diced tomatoes in juice, drained
1 can (28 ounces) crushed tomatoes
2 cups good-quality vegetable stock (available on soup aisle)
1/2 ten-ounce sack triple-washed spinach, stems removed and spinach shredded with knife
Salt and freshly ground black pepper, to taste

Heat a medium soup pot over moderate heat. Add evoo, shallots, and garlic. Sauté 5 minutes. Add diced and crushed tomatoes; stir. Add stock and stir to combine. Stir in spinach in handfuls to wilt it and combine with soup. Season with salt and pepper to taste. Bring soup to a bubble, reduce heat, and simmer 10 to 15 minutes to reduce.

BRUNCHES LUNCHES AND TEA PARTIES, TOO!

51

rachael's TUNA pan bagnat

2 baguettes

1/2 to 2/3 cup (18 to 24 olives) Kalamata olives

2 cans (6.5 ounces each) Italian or French imported tuna in oil, drained (look for this on canned fish or international foods aisles)

1 tin (6 fillets) flat anchovies, drained and chopped

3 tablespoons capers, drained

1/2 red onion, chopped

1 can (15 ounces) artichoke hearts in water, drained and coarsely chopped

1/2 cup drained sun-dried tomatoes in oil, chopped

1/4 to 1/3 cup (a couple handfuls) fresh flat-leaf parsley, chopped

4 or 5 sprigs fresh rosemary, chopped (3 tablespoons)

1 lemon, halved

1 tablespoon red wine vinegar

Coarse black pepper, to taste

3 tablespoons extra-virgin olive oil (evoo) (eyeball it)

Preheat the oven to 400°F.

Crisp baguettes in hot oven, then cool to handle. Cut baguettes in half across, on an angle, then split each half horizontally. Hollow out some of the soft middle to make room for the filling.

If the olives are pitted, coarsely chop them. If the olives have pits, place an olive or two on a cutting board. Place the flat of a knife blade on top of the olives—just like peeling garlic—whack the heel of your hand on the knife and the pits of the olives will be exposed. Remove pits and chop.

Place tuna in a bowl and separate with a fork. Add anchovies, capers, red onions, artichokes, sun-dried tomatoes, olives, parsley, and rosemary.

Squeeze lemon juice into the bowl by holding the lemon halves cut side up, allowing juice to spill over sides (seeds will stay with the lemon half). Add vinegar and pepper and drizzle salad liberally with evoo. Toss to combine and adjust pepper to taste. Pack the tuna salad into hollowed baguette halves and set tops in place. Press down to set the bread and salad together. The bread will absorb the evoo and salad juices. YUMMY! Cut each half baguette in half again, making 8 pieces total.

> **TIP**
>
> To get its juices flowing, place a whole lemon in the microwave on high for 10 seconds.
>
> •
>
> Wrap the sandwich in wax paper, peeling it back as you eat the bagnat. The wrapping will catch extra juices.

30 MINUTE MEALS

MENU

Serves 8

HAVANA LUNCHEON

1

CUBAN-STYLE
PORK TENDERLOIN SANDWICHES
AND FRIED PLANTAINS

2

FROZEN MOJITO SLUSHES

cuban-style PORK tenderloin sandwiches and FRIED PLANTAINS

Put "The Buena Vista Social Club" CD on and invite a few friends over to make a weekend trip to Cuba! Tell them to wear their best cabana shirts, and keep a limbo pole on hand.

Pork Tenderloins

- 1 & 2/3 to 2 pounds pork tenderloin (2 pieces, the average weight of 1 package), trimmed
- Extra-virgin olive oil (evoo) or vegetable oil, for drizzling
- 1 small onion, minced
- 4 cloves garlic, finely chopped
- Grated zest of 2 limes
- Grated zest of 1 large orange
- A handful of fresh flat-leaf parsley, finely chopped
- 1 teaspoon coarse salt
- 1 teaspoon coarse black pepper
- 1 teaspoon dried oregano

Cuban Sweet Rolls

- 8 crusty rolls, such as Portuguese rolls, torpedo loaves, or muffaletta-style round rolls
- 4 teaspoons sugar

Plantains

- 1/4 cup corn oil (4 times around the pan)
- 4 black-skinned plantains
- 1 teaspoon fine salt

Sandwich Fixin's

- 1 pound shaved ham (from the deli counter)
- 1 pound shaved Swiss cheese (from the deli counter)

Relish

- 6 dill pickles, chopped
- 1/2 cup sweet red pepper relish (found on the condiment aisle)
- 2 scallions, chopped

Preheat oven to 425°F.

Prepare the tenderloins: Coat them with evoo. Combine onion, garlic, citrus zest, parsley, salt, and coarse pepper, and oregano in a pile on a cutting board. Pack this coating evenly onto the tenderloins. Place tenderloins on a baking pan and place in hot oven to roast, 20 to 25 minutes. Wash your hands.

TIP
Authentic Cuban rolls for this sandwich are sweet. This sugar wash process gives a similar effect.

Prepare the rolls: Brush rolls with a little warm water and sprinkle with 1/2 teaspoon sugar each. Place on a baking sheet, then in oven with meat for 5 minutes to crust rolls and set sugar. When ready, split and pile on serving plate.

Cook the plantains: Heat 1/4 cup corn oil in a heavy skillet over medium-high heat. Peel plantains and cut in half lengthwise, then slice each half into thirds on an angle. Arrange plantains in pan in a single layer and cook until crisp on each side, about 3 minutes per side. Remove from skillet to a paper towel-lined plate and season with fine salt.

Remove pork from oven and transfer to a cutting board. Let meat rest 5 minutes, then thinly slice meat on an angle. Place ham and Swiss cheese on a serving plate, separating and fluffing up the shaved meat and cheese.

Make the relish: Combine chopped pickles, sweet red pepper relish, and scallions in a small bowl.

Arrange a buffet of relish, meats, cheese, rolls, and plantains. The sandwiches are made with layers of Swiss, ham, pork, and a generous slather of relish. A few slices of plantains per person are eaten as a side dish.

frozen MOJITO slushes

For every 2 slushes, you will need:
1/2 pint lime sorbet **or 1/2 can frozen limeade (from frozen juice section)**
2 shots light rum
1/4 cup mint **leaves**
1/2 tray ice cubes

In a blender, combine all ingredients and pulse, then blend on high until lime-mint slush is smooth. Pour drinks into 2 large cocktail glasses using a long-handled spoon and repeat as necessary. Makes 2 cocktails.

BRUNCHES LUNCHES AND TEA PARTIES, TOO!

Serves 6

BIG BURGER LUNCH

1

BEEFSTEAK TOMATO
AND VIDALIA ONION SALAD WITH
STEAK SAUCE DRESSING

2

OUTSIDE-IN
BACON CHEESEBURGERS WITH
GREEN ONION MAYO

3

KAHLÚA CHOCOLATE CHUNK
COOKIES

kahlúa chocolate chunk COOKIES

1 package (17 & 1/2 ounces) dry chocolate chip cookie mix (found on baking aisle)

7 tablespoons butter, softened

1 large egg, beaten

1/4 cup Kahlúa or other coffee liqueur

3 tablespoons instant espresso or instant coffee crystals

1 tablespoon ground coffee beans

1 cup bittersweet chocolate chunks, such as Ghirardelli brand

4 ounces broken walnut pieces

Preheat oven to 375°F. Place racks in center of oven.

Pour cookie mix into a mixing bowl and make a well in the center. Add softened butter, egg, Kahlúa, instant coffee, ground coffee, chocolate chunks, and walnuts. Mix well to combine all ingredients into cookie dough. Using a small scoop or a heaping teaspoon, drop cookies 2 inches apart on an ungreased nonstick cookie sheet or sheets. Bake cookies in batches, 9 to 11 minutes or until crisp and browned at edges. Transfer to wire rack to cool; serve. Makes 24 cookies.

outside-in BACON CHEESEBURGERS

with green onion mayo

As you bite into the burgers, you will find a smoky, cheesy surprise inside.

6 slices bacon, chopped

4 scallions, cleaned and trimmed

Extra-virgin olive oil (evoo), for drizzling

1 & 3/4 pounds ground beef sirloin

1 & 1/2 tablespoons Worcestershire sauce (eyeball it)

1 & 1/2 tablespoons steak seasoning blend, such as Montreal by McCormick, or coarse salt and fresh black pepper

3/4 pound extra-sharp white cheddar cheese, crumbled

1 cup mayonnaise or reduced-fat mayonnaise

1 teaspoon ground cumin

Salt and freshly ground black pepper, to taste

6 crusty Kaiser rolls, split

6 leaves crisp romaine lettuce

Preheat grill pan over high heat.

In a medium pan, brown bacon and drain on a paper towel–lined plate.

Brush scallions with a little evoo and grill on hot grill pan 2 or 3 minutes on each side. Remove from heat to cool.

Make the burgers: Combine ground beef with Worcestershire and steak seasoning or salt and pepper. Divide meat into 6 equal parts. Combine cheese crumbles and cooked bacon. Take a portion of the ground meat in your hand and make a well in the center of it. Pile in cheese and bacon, then carefully form the burger around the cheese and bacon filling. Make sure the fillings are completely covered with meat. When all 6 large patties are formed, drizzle burgers with evoo and place on hot grill pan. Cook 2 minutes on each side over high heat, reduce heat to medium-low and cook burgers 7 or 8 minutes longer, turning occasionally. Do not press down on burgers as they cook. Transfer to a plate and let them rest 5 minutes before serving.

Make the mayonnaise: Chop cooled, grilled green onions and add to a food processor. Add mayonnaise and cumin and pulse-grind the onions and mayonnaise together. Season with salt and pepper to taste.

Place burgers on crusty buns and top with crisp lettuce leaves and a slather of green onion mayonnaise.

beefsteak TOMATO and vidalia ONION
salad with steak sauce dressing

At Peter Luger's Steak House in Brooklyn, you can order sliced beefsteak tomatoes and thick-cut Vidalia onions. There, you can pour Luger Sauce all over everything—including this salad. This recipe is a quick salad dressing that tastes like tangy steak sauce. Try it on this salad or your next steak!

1/4 cup red wine vinegar (eyeball it)

3 rounded tablespoons brown sugar

1 tablespoon Worcestershire sauce (eyeball it)

1 teaspoon coarse black pepper (eyeball it)

1 cup canned tomato sauce

2 tablespoons extra-virgin olive oil (evoo) (eyeball it)

4 beefsteak tomatoes, sliced 1/2 inch thick

1 large Vidalia onion, peeled and sliced across, 1/2 inch thick

Salt, to taste

3 tablespoons chopped parsley, for garnish

Make the dressing: In a small saucepan over moderate heat combine vinegar, sugar, Worcestershire, and pepper. Allow sugar to dissolve in vinegar and liquids to come to a bubble. Remove sauce from heat and whisk in tomato sauce, then evoo. Serve warm or chilled.

Arrange sliced tomatoes and onions on a serving platter. Season tomatoes and onions with salt. Pour dressing over the tomatoes and onions and garnish with chopped parsley.

30 MINUTE MEALS

MENU

Serves 8

INDOOR BEACH PARTY

1

GRILLED CHICKEN BREASTS AND
LINGUIÇA SAUSAGE

2

WARM CORN AND TOMATO SALAD

3

VICKY'S LITTLENECK CLAMS
WITH PANCETTA, GARLIC, AND WINE

grilled CHICKEN BREASTS
and linguiça SAUSAGE

8 boneless, skinless chicken breasts **(6 to 8 ounces each)**

Grill seasoning, **such as Montreal by McCormick, or salt and coarse pepper to taste**

Juice of 1 lemon

3 tablespoons dry cooking sherry

1/3 cup extra-virgin olive oil **(evoo)**

1 & 1/2 pounds linguiça **sausage**

A handful of chopped fresh flat-leaf parsley

Preheat oven to 375°F.

Preheat a grill pan over high heat. Season chicken with grill seasoning or salt and pepper. Combine lemon, sherry, and evoo in a shallow dish and turn chicken in the mixture to coat evenly. Sear chicken 2 minutes on each side on grill. Transfer to a baking dish and set chicken in oven. Roast chicken for 15 minutes. Add linguiça to hot grill pan and reduce heat to medium-high. Grill 10 minutes to crisp casings and remove from heat. Pile chicken on serving plate and top with parsley. Pile linguiça alongside chicken and serve.

warm CORN AND TOMATO salad

Hot or cold, this corn and tomato salad is so good. It's mayo-free (no need to worry about refrigeration), making it a perfect offering for picnics, tailgating or potluck meals. Add black beans, and serve it as a vegetarian entrée; with added stock, it becomes a quick, thick, and spicy soup. Try it cold, as a salsa with blue corn chips.

2 tablespoons extra-virgin olive oil (evoo) (twice around the pan)

1 small red bell pepper, chopped

1 small green or orange bell pepper, chopped

4 scallions, chopped, whites and greens

3 cloves garlic, chopped

4 cups frozen corn kernels

3 plum tomatoes, seeded and chopped

Juice of 1 lime

1/2 teaspoon ground cumin (eyeball it)

1 tablespoon cayenne pepper sauce (such as Tabasco) (eyeball it)

1 teaspoon sweet paprika (eyeball it)

Coarse salt and freshly ground pepper, to taste

2 tablespoons chopped cilantro or fresh flat-leaf parsley, for garnish

Heat a large nonstick skillet over medium-high heat. Add evoo, peppers, scallions, and garlic. Cook 5 minutes, stirring frequently. Add corn to the pan and allow the liquids from frozen corn to cook out, about 3 minutes. Add tomatoes and lime juice (throw the lime halves right into the pan, too; it will really punch up the flavor). Season with cumin, cayenne sauce, paprika, salt, and pepper. Top with cilantro or parsley and transfer the warm salad to a serving dish.

vicky's LITTLENECK CLAMS
with pancetta, garlic, and wine

This is my best friend Vicky's best recipe for clams.

2 tablespoons extra-virgin olive oil (evoo) (twice around the pan)
4 large cloves garlic, crushed
1/4 pound pancetta, cut into small pieces (available at deli counter)
50 littleneck clams, cleaned
1 cup dry white wine
1/4 cup chopped fresh flat-leaf parsley (a couple handfuls)

Heat a BIG pot with tight-fitting lid over medium-high heat. Add evoo, garlic, and pancetta and brown pancetta for 3 minutes. Add clams to the pot and then the wine. Cover and let the clams steam until they open, 5 to 10 minutes. Discard any unopened shells. Transfer clams and juices to a serving platter and top liberally with parsley. Serve.

Serves 6

HIGH TEA IN LOW COUNTRY

1

SPICY SPIKED ICED TEA

2

ACADIAN-STYLE CRAB SALAD
ON CROISSANTS

3

MISS LESLIE'S
DIVINE HAM SALAD ON BISCUITS

spicy spiked ICED TEA

4 orange Pekoe tea bags

3 cups boiling water

5 to 6 cups ice cubes, plus additional ice to serve

1/3 cup sugar, plus more for serving

Juice of 1 lemon

Juice of 1 orange

1 cinnamon stick

10 whole cloves

6 shots light rum

Lemon wedges, for serving

Place tea bags in a small bowl or large measuring cup. Add 3 cups boiling water and
steep tea 5 minutes.

Fill a large pitcher with ice cubes. Pour sugar over ice. Add lemon and orange juices,
cinnamon stick, and cloves. Pour hot tea over ice and stir with a wooden spoon until
most of the ice dissolves and the tea has cooled. Serve or chill until ready to serve.

When ready to serve, fill tall glasses with ice, add a shot (1 & 1/2 ounces) of light rum to
each. Pour iced tea through a strainer to remove cloves and fruit pulp and pits. Fill
glasses with tea. Serve tea with extra sugar and lemon wedges. Makes 6 servings

BRUNCHES LUNCHES AND TEA PARTIES, TOO!

65

acadian-style CRAB SALAD on croissants

2 tubs (6-ounce) fresh lump crabmeat (1 pound) or 300 count shrimp
   may be substituted

2 stalks celery from the heart, finely chopped

1/4 cup finely chopped or grated white onion

3 tablespoons mayonnaise

1/4 cup chili sauce (eyeball it)

1 teaspoon hot sauce (such as Tabasco)

1 teaspoon Worcestershire sauce

Salt and freshly ground black pepper, to taste

4 leaves Bibb or leaf lettuce

4 large croissants, split

Run your fingers through crabmeat to remove any bits of shell. Add celery, onion, mayo, chili, hot sauce, and Worcestershire. Mix salad with a fork. Season with salt and pepper to taste. Place lettuce leaves on open croissants, pile crab salad on top, and replace croissant top. Cut each into thirds on an angle, following the shape of the pastry. Arrange sandwiches on a plate and serve. Makes 12 pieces.

miss leslie's divine HAM SALAD on biscuits

One great perk that comes along with working in and around food is that you are often surrounded by people who love to cook and eat as much as you do. Serious recipe swapping and swiping occurs as a result. Now, I don't know if Leslie, a co-worker at the network, makes anything of mine at home, but this recipe for her ham salad that she passed on to me is going to be made in my kitchen—frequently!

2 tubes, 6 pieces each, large biscuits (such as Pillsbury brand) (from dairy aisle of market)

1 pound cooked ham, sliced 1/4 inch thick, diced (from the deli)

3 stalks celery, from the heart, finely chopped

1/2 cup salad olives with pimiento, drained and chopped

1 jalapeño pepper, seeded and finely chopped

4 scallions, finely chopped

1/4 cup fresh flat-leaf parsley (a couple handfuls of leaves), finely chopped

1/3 cup mayonnaise (just enough to bind salad)

3 tablespoons prepared yellow mustard

3 tablespoons dill pickle relish

Salt and freshly ground black pepper, to taste

Prepare biscuits to package directions. Cool on a wire rack.

Combine all remaining ingredients in a bowl and adjust seasonings to taste.

Split cool biscuits and fill with Leslie's DEEELICIOUS ham salad. Makes 12 biscuits.

BRUNCHES LUNCHES AND TEA PARTIES,TOO!

30 MINUTE MEALS

MENU

Serves 8

HIGH TEA, LOW MAINTENANCE PARTY

1

SANDWICHES:

SMOKED SALMON ROUNDS

TEA PARTY CLUB SANDWICHES

2

SWEETS:

QUICK CREAM-CURRANT-CRANBERRY SCONES
AND DEVONSHIRE-ISH CREAM

SMOKED SALMON rounds

4 slices pumpernickel bread
2 tablespoons chopped or snipped fresh chives
4 ounces (half a brick) cream cheese, softened
1/2 pound smoked salmon, thinly sliced
2 ounces (1 small jar) salmon roe (optional)
3 tablespoons fresh dill

Lightly toast pumpernickel bread slices. Using a shot glass, a spice jar cap, or other round shape, cut 4 rounds out of each bread slice, 16 rounds total. Mix chives into softened cheese. Spread cream cheese on the rounds in a thin layer. Top each round with a slice of smoked salmon; pile it like a ribbon or roll the slice. Garnish salmon rounds with a dot of salmon roe, if desired, and a sprig of dill. Arrange rounds on a plate.

tea party CLUB SANDWICHES

12 slices white sandwich bread
3/4 cup (1 & 1/2 sticks) sweet cream butter, softened
10 to 12 sprigs tarragon, leaves stripped and chopped (6 tablespoons)
1/2 English (seedless) cucumber, very thinly sliced
1 & 1/2 cups watercress leaves (1 bundle), trimmed
4 plum tomatoes, very thinly sliced
Salt and freshly ground black pepper, to taste

> **TIP**
>
> Also have on hand for High Tea:
>
> •
>
> Teapot(s) and strainers
>
> •
>
> Assorted loose teas, such as: English breakfast, cinnamon, orange, mint, and chamomile
>
> •
>
> Lemon wedges
>
> •
>
> Honey and sugar cubes
>
> •
>
> Shortbread rounds (such as Walker brand)

Trim crusts off of the white bread. Mix butter and tarragon with a rubber spatula. Spread tarragon butter on one side of all 12 slices of bread. On 4 buttered slices, arrange cucumber slices and watercress in thin layers. Top with 4 slices bread, buttered side down. Butter the tops of the 4 completed single-layer sandwiches. Top butter with a layer of sliced tomatoes and season tomatoes with salt and pepper. Complete club sandwiches by setting the remaining 4 slices of bread, buttered side down, on top. Cut sandwiches corner to corner, making 16 triangles. Arrange on a serving plate.

BRUNCHES LUNCHES AND TEA PARTIES, TOO!

69

quick cream-currant-cranberry SCONES and devonshire-ish CREAM

Scones

2 packages (7.5-ounce) complete biscuit mix (such as Bisquick) (3 cups total)

1 cup light cream or half-and-half

1/2 teaspoon grated or ground nutmeg (eyeball it)

1/3 cup currants (2 handfuls)

1/2 cup dried sweetened cranberries (such as Craisins by Ocean Spray)

1/3 cup sugar

1/4 cup (1/2 stick) butter, melted, for brushing

Cream

8 ounces (1 brick) cream cheese, softened

1 teaspoon vanilla

1/4 cup sugar

1/4 cup sour cream

1/4 cup light cream or half-and-half

1 small package edible flowers (available in fresh herbs section of produce department in larger markets) (optional)

Preheat oven to 450°F.

Make the scones: Mix first 6 scone ingredients in a medium bowl. Drop 8 scones each onto 2 nonstick or greased cookie sheets in 2 & 1/2-inch mounds. Brush with melted butter and bake until lightly golden all over, 8 to 11 minutes. Makes 16 scones.

Make the Devonshire-ish Cream: Beat all ingredients together in a medium bowl with a hand mixer. Beat in torn bits of edible flowers, if desired. Transfer sweet, spreadable vanilla cream to a serving dish. Garnish with additional edible flowers, if desired. Makes 2 cups cream.

> **TIP**
>
> Optional accompaniments:
>
> •
>
> Lemon curd (available on jams and preserves aisle)
>
> •
>
> Fresh strawberries

PARTY BITES

LITTLE DISHES WITH BIG TASTE

I entertain with meals more than snacks because I am a big eater and little bites just don't fill me up. Plus, I resist fussing with small things of any kind—from stuffing small mushroom caps to sewing on buttons. I don't have the time or the patience. Yet when friends drop by, just to say hi, I'll put together some delicious party bites quickly. I promise that these recipes are among the least-fussy snacks I've come up with, and they're always good. Still, I suggest you pour yourself a preemptive cocktail, then start your 30-minute party-prep clock. (Now that's what I call a useful tip!)

RACHAEL RAY 30-MINUTE MEALS
gettogethers

Serves 8

A DIP IN THE MEDITERRANEAN

1
•

SAGE SAUSAGE BITES
WITH BALSAMIC APRICOT
MUSTARD DIP

2
•

STOVETOP SPINACH AND
ARTICHOKE DIP
WITH CRUSTY BREAD

3
•

4-MINUTE GARLIC SHRIMP WITH
3-MINUTE FRA DIAVOLO SAUCE

SAGE SAUSAGE BITES
with balsamic apricot mustard dip

1 tablespoon extra-virgin olive oil (evoo) (once around the pan)

1 shallot, chopped

1/4 cup balsamic vinegar (eyeball it)

1 cup apricot all-fruit spread or apricot preserves

1/4 cup spicy brown mustard (3 rounded tablespoonfuls)

1 & 1/4 pounds bulk Italian sweet sausage

3 tablespoons chopped fresh sage (4 or 5 sprigs)

1 cup Italian bread crumbs (a couple handfuls)

Preheat a small pot over medium heat and set the oven to 425°F.

To the pot, add evoo and shallot and sauté 1 minute. Next add balsamic vinegar and reduce by half, 1 minute. Remove from heat and combine with apricot all-fruit spread or preserves and spicy mustard. Stir until mustard is fully incorporated; dip will be glossy and brown in color. Place dip in a small serving bowl.

In a mixing bowl, combine sweet sausage and chopped sage. Add 2 tablespoonfuls of apricot dip and mix. Break meat into bite-size nuggets, coat in bread crumbs, then place on a nonstick cookie sheet. Bake 10 to 12 minutes, until evenly browned, turning occasionally. Drain, then serve with party picks for dipping in balsamic apricot dip. Makes 20 to 24 pieces.

Suggested beverages: Italian beer (Moretti, Peroni) and wines (Chianti Classico, Primitivo, Nero d'Avola) and San Pellegrino water and sliced citrus fruit

---

TIP

To round out the party:

•

Get a variety of Italian cheeses cheeses, 1/2 pound of each. I like going from a fontina, mild and creamy, to a table cheese, like a sheep's milk cheese with black pepper, on to a pungent blue, like a creamy Gorgonzola. Set the whole pieces of cheese on a cutting board with pears and grapes alongside them.

•

Hazelnuts

•

Olives

•

Celery hearts

•

Assorted bread sticks

PARTY BITES LITTLE DISHES WITH BIG TASTE

73

stovetop SPINACH and ARTICHOKE DIP with crusty bread

2 tablespoons extra-virgin olive oil (evoo) (twice around the pan)

1 tablespoon butter

3 cloves garlic, chopped

1 small yellow onion, chopped

2 tablespoons chopped fresh thyme (a few sprigs) or 2 teaspoons dried

1/2 small red bell pepper, seeded and chopped

2 tablespoons all-purpose flour

1/2 cup dry white wine

1 cup chicken or vegetable stock

1/2 cup half-and-half or heavy cream

1 can (15 ounces) artichoke hearts in water, drained and coarsely chopped

2 boxes (10 ounces each) frozen chopped spinach, defrosted and squeezed dry in a kitchen towel

1 & 1/2 cups shredded Italian 4-cheese blend (provolone, Parmesan, mozzarella, and Asiago) (available in 10-ounce sacks on the dairy aisle)

Salt and freshly ground black pepper, to taste

1 round loaf crusty bread, top removed and cubed, bottom hollowed out to use as serving bowl

1 loaf multigrain or whole wheat baguette, sliced at bakery/bread counter in market

To a medium saucepan preheated over moderate heat, add about 2 tablespoons evoo in a slow stream. Add butter to evoo. When butter has melted, add garlic and onions to the pot. Sprinkle in thyme leaves. Sauté, 2 minutes; add red pepper. Sauté mixture a minute more. Sprinkle in flour, stir to coat vegetables. Cook, 1 minute. Whisk in wine and reduce by half. Whisk in stock and thicken sauce, 1 minute. Stir in half-and-half or cream. When sauce returns to a bubble, add artichokes, spinach, and cheese. Keep stirring until cheese melts and sauce is well combined. Add salt and pepper and adjust seasonings to your taste.

Pour dip into hollow bread bowl on serving platter and surround with sliced multi- or whole-grain bread for dipping. Reserve extra dip to warm and refill as necessary. Cut up bread bowl when baguette slices are gone—the bowl is the best part, as it absorbs juices from the dip.

4-minute GARLIC SHRIMP
with 3-minute FRA DIAVOLO SAUCE

2 tablespoons extra-virgin olive oil (evoo) (twice around the pan)

4 cloves garlic, crushed away from skin

24 jumbo shrimp, peeled and deveined, tails intact (ask for easy-peels at seafood counter)

2 teaspoons grill or steak seasoning blend, such as Montreal Seasoning by McCormick, or coarse salt and freshly ground black pepper, to taste

Sauce

2 tablespoons extra-virgin olive oil (evoo) (twice around the pan)

1/2 teaspoon crushed red pepper flakes

2 shallots, chopped

1/2 cup dry sherry or dry white wine

1 can (15 ounces) crushed tomatoes

Salt and freshly ground black pepper, to taste

2 tablespoons chopped parsley (a handful)

TIP

The Setup:

•

I serve nuts, like the hazelnuts in this menu, out of brandy snifters. Guests spill nuts into their hand to snack on.

•

Olives are easy party fare, but remember to put out an extra, small dish near olives to collect the pits.

•

Trim celery hearts at the root and place them in water glass, the leafy tops sticking out. Present the assorted breadsticks in the same manner.

Make the shrimp: Heat a large skillet over medium-high heat. Add evoo, garlic, and shrimp. Season with grill seasoning or salt and pepper, and cook shrimp, 3 minutes or until just pink. Remove shrimp to a serving platter.

Make the sauce: Return pan to heat, and add 2 tablespoons evoo. Pick garlic cloves out of the shrimp, chop them coarsely and return to pot. Add crushed red pepper and shallots. Add sherry or white wine, and reduce by half, 1 minute. Add tomatoes and bring to a bubble, 1 minute. Season sauce with salt and pepper and stir in parsley. Transfer sauce to a small bowl and place next to cooked shrimp.

PARTY BITES LITTLE DISHES WITH BIG TASTE

MENU

Serves 8

A TASTY TOASTY CROSTINI PARTY

1

GARLIC TOASTS

2

TOPPINGS:

TUNA AND OLIVE TAPENADE

ITALIAN DEVILED EGG SPREAD

RICOTTA AND OLIVE SPREAD

SLICED ROMA TOMATOES AND
MARINATED BOCCONCINI

ARUGULA WITH SHAVED PARMIGIANO
AND PROSCIUTTO

ROASTED GARLIC HUMMUS WITH ROSEMARY

garlic toasts for CROSTINI

1/2 cup extra-virgin olive oil (evoo) (eyeball it)
2 cloves garlic, crushed
2 baguettes, sliced at bakery counter

Preheat oven to 375°F.

Start toasts, and work on other dishes while bread is toasting in the oven: Place evoo and garlic in a small pot or in a microwave-safe dish. Heat over medium-low heat for 2 or 3 minutes or microwave with a loose plastic cover for 20 seconds on high. Remove oil from heat or microwave oven.

Place 2 cookie sheets on the counter. Pour about 1/4 cup garlic oil onto each cookie sheet. Place sliced bread onto each sheet, as much as will fill the trays in a single layer. Toss bread with garlic oil to coat, and spread into single layers on each sheet. Place toasts in the oven and bake 10 minutes or until bread is evenly toasted and crisp.

Place toasts in a big basket, and set on buffet to be surrounded by toppings. Makes about 60 toasts

PARTY BITES LITTLE DISHES WITH BIG TASTE

3 GREAT TOPPERS:

italian deviled egg spread, ricotta and olive spread,
tuna and olive tapenade

6 large eggs

2 cups low-moisture, part-skim ricotta cheese

1/2 cup drained green olives with pimiento or salad olives (chopped
  green olives and pimiento)

2 or 3 cloves garlic, cracked away from skin

2 tins (6 ounces each) Italian tuna in oil, drained

4 anchovy fillets

1/4 red onion, coarsely chopped

A handful fresh flat-leaf parsley leaves

1 cup pitted Kalamata black olives (available in bulk bins near deli section)

Juice of 1/2 lemon

Salt and freshly ground black pepper, to taste

2 teaspoons Worcestershire sauce (eyeball it—several drops)

2 rounded teaspoons prepared mustard, such as Dijon

3 rounded tablespoons mayonnaise

1/2 teaspoon crushed red pepper flakes

3 tablespoons capers

1/4 small white onion, finely chopped

Start the deviled egg spread: Place eggs in a small pot and cover with water. Place over
  high heat and bring the water to a boil.

While eggs are cooking, make the ricotta spread: In a food processor, combine ricotta,
  green olives and pimientos, and 2 cloves of garlic. Process to a smooth spread.
  Scrape into a bowl and refrigerate until ready to serve. Rinse out processor bowl,
  and return it to processor base.

When eggs come to a boil, cover the pot, remove from heat, and let stand, 10 minutes.

Meanwhile, make the tapenade: Place tuna, anchovies, red onion, parsley, Kalamata
  olives, lemon juice, and some black pepper in food processor. Pulse-grind
  ingredients into a coarse spread, and transfer to a serving dish.

Run eggs under cold water to quick-cool. Peel and coarsely chop the eggs. Combine
  with Worcestershire, mustard, mayo, crushed pepper flakes, capers, and onion.
  Season with salt and pepper to taste, and transfer to a small serving dish.

3 MORE TOPPINGS IN 5 MINUTES FLAT: sliced roma tomatoes and marinated bocconcini, arugula with shaved parmigiano and prosciutto, roasted garlic hummus with rosemary

4 Roma tomatoes, sliced

Coarse salt, to taste

1 tub marinated bocconcini (mozzarella bites) (available in tubs in specialty cheese case of market)

1 sack (5 ounces) ready-to-use arugula

Juice of 1/2 lemon

Extra-virgin olive oil (evoo), for drizzling

1/4 pound Parmigiano Reggiano cheese

1/3 pound sliced prosciutto

2 cups store-bought roasted garlic hummus

3 tablespoons chopped fresh rosemary leaves (4 or 5 sprigs)

1 teaspoon crushed red pepper flakes

Prepare the bocconcini: Spread tomato slices on a serving plate. Sprinkle with a little salt. Remove the bocconcini from the liquid with a slotted spoon, and place alongside the tomatoes. To eat, place a slice of tomato on a crostini toast, and top with a piece of a bocconcini.

Prepare the arugula: Coarsely chop arugula, and toss with lemon juice and evoo to coat. Season with a little salt and toss with your fingertips. Using a vegetable peeler, garnish with shavings of cheese. Place serving tongs in arugula. Loosely pile sliced prosciutto on a small plate, and serve alongside the greens. To eat, guests put a bit of greens and cheese on toast, and top with a piled-up slice of prosciutto.

Make the hummus: Mix hummus with chopped fresh rosemary in a small bowl, and garnish the top with a teaspoon of crushed red pepper flakes. Place a spreader or spoon in hummus, and serve.

PARTY BITES · LITTLE DISHES WITH BIG TASTE

30 MINUTE MEALS

Serves 8

TAPAS PARTY

1
•

BLOODY MARIAS

2
•

TASTY TAPAS:

CRUSTY BREAD

SLICED TOMATOES WITH LEMON

SLICED PIMIENTOS

SPANISH CHEESE AND MIXED OLIVES

GRILLED CHORIZO

SHERRY-GARLIC BEEF AND MUSHROOMS

BLOODY MARIAS

2 quarts tomato-vegetable juice (such as V-8)

Juice of 2 limes

2 teaspoons coarsely ground black pepper (eyeball it)

1 to 2 tablespoons hot sauce (such as Tabasco), to taste

8 to 10 shots good-quality tequila

8 celery stalks, from the heart

16 jumbo pimiento-stuffed cocktail olives

8 ten- to twelve-inch bamboo skewers

Combine first 5 ingredients in a pitcher and chill. Cut celery into 2-inch pieces and skewer along with olives, using 4 chunks of celery and 2 large olives per skewer. To serve, place a skewer into a tall glass and add ice. Pour Bloody Maria down over ice to fill glass. The celery and olives make a tasty snack when you get to the bottom!

TIP

Other suggested beverages:

•

White and red Rioja wines

•

Sparkling water with slices of citrus

TASTY TAPAS: crusty bread, sliced tomatoes with lemon, sliced pimientos, spanish cheese and mixed olives

1 loaf (24 inches or longer) crusty bread

2 or 3 large cloves garlic, crushed

Extra-virgin olive oil (evoo), for drizzling

4 small to medium vine-ripe tomatoes

Juice of 1 lemon

Coarse salt, to taste

4 whole pimiento peppers, drained (found in glass jars with Spanish and Mexican foods)

1 & 1/4 pounds manchego cheese

2 cups assorted large olives, green and black stuffed or pitted, mixed

3-inch party picks

Preheat broiler to high.

Cut bread in half then slit loaf lengthwise. Char the bread under the broiler, then rub with crushed garlic and drizzle with evoo. Cut bread into large, bite-size cubes and transfer to a basket.

Slice tomatoes and arrange on a platter. Dress with lemon juice and salt.

Slice pimientos and place in a small serving dish. Slice or cube half of the manchego, leave the remainder whole with a utensil to cut with alongside. Serve on a cutting board. Place olives in a dish near cheese.

TIP

Use party picks to stack tomatoes and/or cheese and olives with bread cubes to pop into your mouth. Bread cubes are also tasty with Sherry-Garlic Beef and Mushrooms.

MORE TASTY TAPAS: grilled chorizo, sherry-garlic beef and mushrooms

1/2 cup fresh flat-leaf parsley leaves (a couple handfuls)

8 cloves garlic, cracked away from skin

1 pound chorizo sausage, casings trimmed away

1/4 cup extra-virgin olive oil (evoo)

1 & 1/2 pounds tenderloin or beef sirloin, well trimmed, cut into bite-size pieces

Coarse salt and freshly ground black pepper, to taste

1 cup dry sherry

24 medium to large mushroom caps

Preheat a grill pan over medium-high heat.

Place parsley and garlic in a food processor and chop.

Heat a large, heavy skillet over high heat.

Cut chorizo on an angle in 1/2-inch slices. Grill 2 minutes on each side. Transfer to a serving dish.

Prepare the beef: To the hot skillet, add about 2 tablespoons evoo. Add beef and sear the pieces on all sides to caramelize it evenly. Add half of the garlic and parsley mixture to the pan. Turn to coat the meat. Season meat with salt and pepper. Add 1/2 cup sherry and turn the meat in the wine as it deglazes the pan. Transfer to a serving dish and cover with loose foil to keep warm. Return pan to heat.

Repeat the same process with the mushrooms: Add 2 tablespoons evoo to the pan; add mushrooms, cook 3 or 4 minutes to char edges and soften. Add parsley and garlic, then salt and pepper, then sherry. Reduce sherry while scraping up pan drippings and remove to a separate serving dish.

PARTY BITES LITTLE DISHES WITH BIG TASTE

30 MINUTE MEALS

MENU

Serves 8

SNACK ATTACK PARTY

1

GRILLED POLENTA
CRACKERS WITH ROASTED
RED PEPPER SALSA

2

RACHAEL'S CHIMICHURRI
CHICKEN BITES

3

LAVASH PIZZAS WITH
SMOKED CHEESE AND HAM

grilled POLENTA CRACKERS
with roasted red pepper salsa

1 tube (18 ounces) store-bought polenta, plain or sun dried tomato flavor, cut into 1/2-inch slices

1/4 cup extra-virgin olive oil (evoo) (eyeball it)

3 roasted red peppers (16-ounce jar), drained well

1/2 cup Kalamata black olives, pitted

2 tablespoons capers

1/2 cup fresh flat-leaf parsley leaves (a couple handfuls)

1/4 red onion

1 to 2 cloves garlic

1/2 teaspoon crushed red pepper flakes

Preheat grill pan to high.

Brush polenta slices lightly with evoo. Grill 2 or 3 minutes on each side to score the "crackers" and warm them.

Place peppers, olives, capers, parsley, onion, garlic, and red pepper flakes in a food processor and pulse to chop salsa. Top polenta with spoonfuls of salsa and serve.

PARTY BITES LITTLE DISHES WITH BIG TASTE

rachael's CHIMICHURRI chicken bites

This recipe is my take on chimichurri: oil, vinegar, onions, garlic, herbs, and spices—to serve as both marinade and dipping sauce.

2 serrano or jalapeño peppers

1 rounded tablespoon sweet paprika

1/2 cup fresh flat-leaf parsley leaves (a couple handfuls)

3 tablespoons fresh oregano leaves (4 sprigs)

3 tablespoons fresh thyme leaves (5 or 6 sprigs)

2 bay leaves, crumbled

1/2 small white onion, coarsely chopped

3 cloves garlic

1 cup extra-virgin olive oil (evoo) (eyeball it)

3 tablespoons red wine vinegar (3 splashes)

1 teaspoon coarse salt

1 & 1/2 to 1 & 3/4 pounds chicken tenders

Preheat a grill pan over high heat.

Char peppers by holding over a gas flame or placing under the broiler for 1 to 2 minutes to blister them all over. Seed and coarsely chop the peppers and place in a food processor. Add paprika, herbs, onion, and garlic. Finely chop the mixture by pulsing the power. Transfer to a bowl and stir in evoo, vinegar, and salt. Taste to adjust seasonings.

Cut chicken tenders into thirds and place in a shallow dish. Wash your hands.

Spoon half of the chimichurri over the chicken and coat completely and evenly. Using tongs, transfer the chicken bites to the hot grill and cook, 2 or 3 minutes on each side. Transfer bites to a serving plate. Serve with party picks and reserved chimichurri sauce for dipping.

LAVASH PIZZAS

with smoked cheese and ham

1 package lavash flat bread, plain or flavored
Extra-virgin olive oil (evoo), for drizzling
1 pound smoked mozzarella, diced into small cubes (28 to 32 pieces)
1/4 pound prosciutto, cut into 1/2 inch strips
1 cup arugula leaves (a couple handfuls), chopped
Freshly ground black pepper, to taste

Preheat oven to 375°F.

Cover 2 cookie sheets with lavash. Drizzle lavash with little evoo and turn over. Dot lavash with cubes of smoked mozzarella, spacing 1 inch apart. Make rows of cheese dots down and across the flat bread.

Place bread in oven to melt cheese, 5 minutes. Remove from oven and top with ham strips, draping them over the cheese. Scatter chopped arugula over the pizza. Cut into squares and drizzle with evoo and season with black pepper. Transfer to plate and serve.

TIP

To fill out menu:

•

Assorted gourmet potato chips (herb and garlic or onion flavors)

•

Store-bought hummus, any variety

•

Suggested beverages:

•

San Pellegrino

•

Italian sodas and mineral water

•

Imported beer selections

PARTY BITES LITTLE DISHES WITH BIG TASTE

87

Serves 8

LITE BITES PARTY

1
•

LEMON PEPPER
CHICKEN TENDERS

2
•

CHICKPEA AND ROSEMARY DIP
WITH ZUCCHINI "CHIPS"

3
•

SPINACH- AND ARTICHOKE-STUFFED
PORTOBELLOS

Your friends will love you for this healthy, great-tasting party menu. The lemon pepper chicken is cooked with olive oil and the dip replaces fattening cream cheese and sour cream spreads normally passed at parties. The mushrooms have a little cheese, but no sausage or rich crabmeat, and the stuffing is held together with broth not butter. It's all figure-friendly, easy to make, and oh, so good.

lemon pepper CHICKEN TENDERS

Zest and juice of 2 lemons
1/3 cup extra-virgin olive oil (evoo) (eyeball it)
2 pounds chicken breast tenders (20 pieces)
Salt and coarsely ground black pepper, to taste
20 six-inch bamboo skewers

Heat a large nonstick skillet, grill pan, or indoor grill to medium-high heat. In a shallow dish, combine lemon zest and juice with evoo. Season chicken with salt. Pour half of the marinade over chicken and reserve half. Turn chicken in marinade to coat lightly. Cook tenders in 2 batches, in a single layer in a very hot skillet or grill, 3 minutes on each side, while basting occasionally with reserved marinade. Transfer chicken to a serving platter, place skewers alongside.

chickpea and rosemary DIP with zucchini "CHIPS"

2 cans (15 ounces each) chickpeas (garbanzo beans), drained
1 small jar (6 ounces) roasted red peppers, drained and coarsely chopped
Juice of 1/2 lemon
2 cloves garlic, cracked away from skin
4 stems fresh rosemary, leaves stripped from stems
Coarse salt and freshly ground black pepper, to taste
2 tablespoons extra-virgin olive oil (evoo) (eyeball it)
1 package "everything"-flavor flat breads
1 pint grape tomatoes
1 zucchini, sliced into 1/8-inch discs

Combine chickpeas, roasted red pepper, lemon juice, garlic, rosemary, salt, and pepper in a food processor. Turn the processor on and stream in evoo. Remove spread to a serving bowl and surround with flat breads, grape tomatoes, and zucchini.

PARTY BITES   LITTLE DISHES WITH BIG TASTE

89

spinach- and artichoke-stuffed
PORTOBELLOS

Portobellos

2 teaspoons extra-virgin olive oil (evoo) (a drizzle)

5 medium portobello mushroom caps

Salt and freshly ground black pepper, to taste

2 tablespoons balsamic vinegar

Stuffing

1 tablespoon extra-virgin olive oil (evoo) (once around the pan)

3 cloves garlic, chopped

1 small yellow onion, chopped

1 pound fresh spinach, coarsely chopped

1 can (15 ounces) artichoke hearts in water (6 to 8 count), drained well on paper towels

Salt and freshly ground black pepper, to taste

4 to 6 sprigs fresh thyme, leaves stripped and chopped (about 2 tablespoons)

3 slices Italian bread, toasted and chopped into small cubes

1 cup chicken or vegetable stock

1/4 cup grated Parmesan cheese (a handful)

6 ounces fontina cheese, shredded

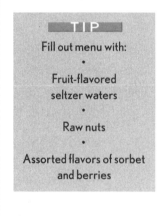

TIP

Fill out menu with:

•

Fruit-flavored
seltzer waters

•

Raw nuts

•

Assorted flavors of sorbet
and berries

Preheat oven to 400°F.

Prepare the mushroom caps: Heat a large nonstick skillet over medium-high heat. Add a drizzle of evoo and the mushroom caps. Season caps with salt and pepper, and cook 3 minutes on each side. Add balsamic to the pan and allow the vinegar to cook away as it coats the caps. Transfer balsamic-glazed caps to a cookie sheet.

Make the stuffing: Return pan to the stove and add evoo, garlic, and onion. Sauté onions and garlic, 3 minutes; add spinach to the pan and let it wilt. Coarsely chop artichoke hearts and add to the spinach. Season veggies with salt, pepper, and thyme. Add chopped toast and dampen stuffing with chicken or vegetable stock. Combine stuffing and sprinkle in a little grated cheese. Top each mushroom with 1/5 of the stuffing and sprinkle lightly with a few strands of fontina. Set mushrooms in oven for 5 minutes to set the mushrooms and melt the cheese strands. Cut each mushroom into 4 pieces and transfer to a serving dish.

GREAT DATES

ROMANTIC MENUS FOR TWO

I've said it before: the way to anyone's heart is through his (her) stomach. Even if you cannot boil water, you burn the entrée (and the entrée was meat, but your date is vegetarian), aliens land and steal the food to study it and leave you with nothing but a pile of green space rocks to serve—even if all that happens, YOU will still impress your date, simply because you tried to do something special just for him (her). Show how much you care through cooking. And if you keep those pots rocking, your date will keep on knocking...at your door!

RACHAEL RAY 30-MINUTE MEALS
gettogethers

30 MINUTE MEALS

MENU

Serves 2

SEDUCTIVE SUPPER

1
●

ASPARAGUS VELVET SOUP

2
●

LOBSTER TAILS
THERMIDOR

3
●

BERRY-MI-SU
(BERRY-ME-UP)

ASPARAGUS velvet soup

1 bundle (about 20 spears) thin spears asparagus

1/2 cup dry white wine

1/2 cup water

2 tablespoons butter

2 tablespoons flour

1 & 1/2 cups good-quality vegetable stock (available on soup aisle)

Salt and white pepper, to taste

1/2 cup heavy whipping cream

1 tablespoon chopped fresh tarragon or chives, for garnish (optional)

Edible flowers, for garnish (optional)

Trim asparagus by holding a spear at both ends and allowing it to snap. Use this spear as a guide to cut away the tough ends of the rest.

Bring wine and water to a simmer, add asparagus. Cook, covered, 5 minutes or until tender. Drain asparagus liquid into a food processor. Cut tips off asparagus on an angle and reserve them. Cut the remaining spears into 1-inch pieces and purée in food processor with cooking liquid.

In a medium saucepan, melt butter over medium heat. Whisk in flour and cook 2 minutes. Whisk in stock and bring liquid to a bubble. Whisk in asparagus stock and return soup to a bubble. Season soup with salt and pepper and stir in cream. Cook to thicken soup slightly. Adjust seasonings and serve hot in small or shallow bowls topped with reserved asparagus tips, chopped herbs and/or edible flower for garnish.

TIP

Floating an edible flower in each bowl of soup makes a special garnish that adds subtle fragrance (found in packages in produce section, near fresh herbs)

GREAT DATES ROMANTIC MENUS FOR TWO

LOBSTER TAILS thermidor

2 packaged (8-ounce) lobster tails, **or 1 pound jumbo shrimp or prawns**

4 tablespoons butter, **divided**

1/2 small white onion, **finely chopped**

2 tablespoons flour

A splash of dry white wine **or dry sherry**

1/2 cup milk **(eyeball it)**

1/3 cup grated white cheddar **cheese**

1/2 teaspoon paprika **or Old Bay seasoning**

Salt **and freshly ground black** pepper, **to taste**

2 tablespoons Parmesan **cheese**

2 tablespoons bread crumbs

A handful fresh flat-leaf parsley **leaves mixed with 2 cups baby greens, for garnish**

1 lemon, **cut into wedges, for garnish**

Bring a pot of water, 3 or 4 inches deep, to a boil. Add lobster tails to the water and boil 7 to 8 minutes. Drain and shock under cold water to cool. Use kitchen scissors to cut away soft underside of tails. Save the shells, arranging them in a shallow casserole dish. Chop the cooked meat on an angle into chunks.

Preheat the broiler to high.

Heat a medium skillet and a small saucepan over medium heat. To the small saucepan, melt 2 tablespoons butter. Add onion and cook 3 to 5 minutes until very soft. To the skillet, add the remaining 2 tablespoons butter. When the butter melts, add chopped lobster meat and sauté.

Add flour to saucepan with onions and cook together another minute or two. Whisk in wine or sherry, then milk. Remove sauce from heat and stir in cheddar cheese and paprika or Old Bay. Season sauce with salt and pepper. Pour sauce over lobster meat and stir to combine. Pour lobster into and over the shells in a casserole dish and top with Parmesan cheese and bread crumbs. Broil on high until golden, 2 or 3 minutes. Serve each tail, spilling over with lobster bits in sauce, on a bed of mixed baby greens and parsley with wedges of lemon alongside.

To make this dish with jumbo shrimp, cut up peeled, deveined raw shrimp. Sauté the shrimp in butter, as with

TIP
Substitute mixed cooked crab and shrimp for lobster meat for Seafood Thermidor.

94

cooked lobster. Cook until pink and firm and proceed with recipe. Place the shrimp and sauce into a small casserole, then spoon completed shrimp Thermidor over bed of greens and parsley leaves.

BERRY-MI-SU (berry-me-up)

1/2 package ladyfingers **sponge cakes**
1 cup raspberries
4 large strawberries, **sliced**
1/2 cup fresh blackberries **(a couple handfuls)**
Juice of 1 lemon
2 tablespoons sugar
1 cup mascarpone cheese **(available in specialty cheese case of supermarket)**
1/3 cup heavy cream
1/3 cup confectioners' sugar

Open the ladyfingers and separate them.

Combine raspberries with sliced strawberries and blackberries. Toss with lemon juice and sugar.

Line 2 large martini glasses or glass dessert bowls with a single layer of ladyfingers, letting the cakes overlap a bit at the stem. Press the cakes down a bit to fit the lines of the glass. Cover the cake with berries. With a hand mixer, beat cheese with cream and sugar on low, 2 minutes. Spoon sweetened cheese over berries. Spoon more berries over sweetened cheese. Top glasses off with a cap of the ladyfingers dotted with berry juice and more mixed berries.

Serves 2 Couples

ROOFTOP SUPPER FOR 4

1
•

VEGETABLE
ANTIPASTO-STUFFED BREAD

2
•

GRILLED ROSEMARY
TUNA STEAKS WITH
EGGPLANT AND ZUCCHINI SALSA

3
•

BERRIES AND SWEET CREAM

My true love, John, has a typical NYC apartment: hip, but oh so small. The ceilings are high, the light is great, but by far the biggest thing going for this little pad is that it opens up to a rooftop. His little piece of black-topped brick is a real slice of heaven on earth—magical and, in fact, lush. I love how close we have to be to cook together in the tiny kitchen-built-for-two that overlooks the living space. But when the meal is ready, until that first snowfall, you will find us at the metal café table among his roses, under the Tuscan olive tree, up on the roof. The table sits four, and dinner partners are under constant recruitment.

I designed this meal for us to share with the lovely Gina Glickman and her beau, Rick. Gina likes lots of veggies and fish. Add a candle or two, and this is a romantic Mediterranean get-together that you can make any night of the week.

vegetable antipasto-stuffed BREAD

1 loaf crusty bread, 9 to 12 inches in length/diameter

1/4 cup fresh flat-leaf parsley, chopped (a couple handfuls)

1/4 cup (half a small jar) sun-dried tomatoes in olive oil, drained, chopped

1/4 cup black pitted Kalamata or oil-cured olives, chopped

1/2 cup prepared pesto, store-bought or homemade

1/4 pound deli-sliced provolone cheese

1 jar (14 ounces) roasted red peppers, drained

1 can (15 ounces) quartered artichoke hearts in water, drained

1 cup chopped giardiniera (pickled vegetables: hot peppers, cauliflower, carrots) (available on the Italian foods aisle of market or in bulk bins near deli section with bulk olives)

Juice of 1/2 lemon

Coarse salt and freshly ground black pepper, to taste

Extra-virgin olive oil (evoo), for drizzling

1/2 a sack mixed greens, from produce section (3 loosely packed cups)

Cut the top off a loaf of crusty bread. Hollow out the inside of the bread.

Mix parsley, sun-dried tomatoes, olives, and pesto. Spread the mixture evenly across the bottom of the hollowed-out bread. Layer the cheese into the loaf. Layer the roasted red peppers on top of the cheese. Coarsely chop the artichoke hearts and add them in a layer over the red peppers. Sprinkle in the pickled vegetables. Coat the greens with lemon, salt, and pepper and a generous drizzle of evoo. Pile the greens on top of the filled loaf and replace the top. Cut the stuffed loaf into pieces and serve.

grilled rosemary TUNA STEAKS
with eggplant and zucchini SALSA

4 tuna steaks (6 to 8 ounces each)
1 &1/2 tablespoons balsamic vinegar (enough to lightly coat steaks)
6 sprigs fresh rosemary, stripped and chopped (about 3 tablespoons)
Steak seasoning blend such as Montreal Seasoning by McCormick, or coarse salt and freshly ground black pepper, to taste
Extra-virgin olive oil (evoo), for drizzling (about 2 tablespoons)

Salsa

2 tablespoons extra-virgin olive oil (evoo) (twice around the pan)
4 cloves garlic, chopped
1 medium onion, chopped
1 small zucchini
1 small yellow squash
1 small, young, firm eggplant
6 sprigs fresh thyme, chopped (2 tablespoons)
Salt and freshly ground black pepper, to taste
2 small vine-ripe tomatoes, seeded and diced

Prepare the fish: Preheat a grill pan to high or preheat grill or charcoal. Coat tuna in vinegar and rub with rosemary, and steak seasoning blend, or salt and pepper. Drizzle fish with oil, coating lightly on both sides.

Make the salsa: Preheat a medium nonstick skillet over medium-high heat. Add evoo in a slow stream. Add garlic and onion, and sauté, 2 or 3 minutes. Dice zucchini and squash while the onion begins to soften. Add zucchini and squash to the pan and turn to coat and combine with garlic and onion.

Slice eggplant into strips and dice, then add to the pan. Turn to combine all of the vegetables. Add thyme, salt, and pepper to season the mixture. Cook over medium-high heat, stirring frequently, 10 minutes, until vegetables are just fork-tender.

Grill tuna 2 to 3 minutes on each side for rare, up to 6 minutes on each side for well done.

When tuna is done and vegetables are fork-tender, stir chopped tomatoes into eggplant and zucchini mixture and remove vegetables from heat.

TIP

A nice chilled Sicilian rosé, makes a fine beverage companion.

Serve wedges of Vegetable Antipasto-Stuffed Bread, alongside tuna steaks topped with vegetable salsa. Extra antipasto slices and vegetables should be passed at the table.

BERRIES and sweet cream

- **1/2 pint** blackberries
- **1/2 pint** raspberries **or sliced strawberries**
- **2 teaspoons** sugar
- **2 ounces** anisette **(licorice-flavored liqueur, such as Sambuca Romano)**
- **1 pint** vanilla ice cream
- **Store-bought real** whipped cream **in a spray can (from dairy aisle of market)**
- **8 pizzelle** cookies **(found on packaged cookies aisle), or wafer cookies**

Combine berries with sugar and liqueur. Spoon berries into cocktail glasses or dessert cups, reserving a few for garnish. Top with small scoops of ice cream and a rosette of whipped cream. Garnish with a few remaining berries and serve with pizzelle or wafer cookies.

30
MINUTE
MEALS

MENU

Serves 2

A GET AWAY FOR ANY DAY BAJA BLOWOUT

1

MUSSELS
IN MEXICAN BEER

2

HECK OF A JICAMA SALAD

3

CHORIZO AND SHRIMP
QUESADILLAS WITH SMOKY
GUACAMOLE

This menu is a jazzed-up home version of a great date John and I had out at a Mexican restaurant in NYC. When we make it ourselves, it's even more romantic; it's like getting away to Baja for the evening.

MUSSELS in mexican beer

Simple, delish, and ready in less than 10 minutes, this recipe may be made first if you enjoy mouthfuls of mussels while you cook. John and I make it last, right before we sit down. We feast and snuggle our way through date nights all week long. Spoiled rotten, we are.

2 tablespoons extra-virgin olive oil (evoo) (twice around the pan)

4 cloves garlic, cracked away from skin and crushed

1 small onion, chopped

1 jalapeño, seeded and chopped

A couple pinches salt

2 dozen mussels, scrubbed

1/2 cup dark Mexican beer, such as Negro Modelo or Dos Equis

1 can (15 ounces), diced tomatoes, drained

2 tablespoons chopped fresh flat-leaf parsley or cilantro

In a deep skillet with a cover preheated over medium-high heat, add evoo, garlic, onion and jalapeño. Season with salt. Sauté 2 minutes. Arrange mussels in the pan. Pour in beer and tomatoes and shake the pan to combine. Cover pan and cook 3 to 5 minutes or until mussels open. Remove from heat and spoon sauce down into shells. Garnish with parsley or cilantro. Serve immediately from the pan.

GREAT DATES ROMANTIC MENUS FOR TWO

heck of a JICAMA SALAD

1/2 bulb jicama root, **peeled and sliced into thick matchsticks**
1/2 teaspoon salt
2 teaspoons sugar
Juice of 2 limes
2 hearts of romaine **lettuce, chopped**
2 tablespoons finely chopped cilantro **(a handful of leaves)**
1/2 teaspoon cumin **(eyeball it in the palm of your hand)**
3 tablespoons extra-virgin olive oil **(evoo) (eyeball it)**
Fresh black pepper, **to taste**

Place jicama in a bowl, sprinkle with salt and sugar, then cover with cold water. Add the juice of 1 lime. Let jicama stand 15 minutes, then drain well. While jicama soaks, work on the rest of the meal.

After 15 minutes, arrange the romaine on a serving plate. Top with drained jicama. Juice 1 lime into a small bowl, add cilantro and cumin. Whisk in evoo in a slow stream. Pour dressing over salad and season with salt and pepper.

chorizo and shrimp QUESADILLAS
with smoky guacamole

Guacamole

2 ripe Haas avocados

Juice of 1 lime

A couple pinches salt

1/4 cup sour cream (3 rounded tablespoonfuls)

2 chipotle peppers in adobo (available in cans on specialty food aisle in Mexican section of market)

Quesadillas

1/2 pound chorizo sausage, sliced thin on an angle

1 tablespoon extra-virgin olive oil (evoo), plus some for drizzling

1 clove garlic, cracked away from skin and crushed

12 large shrimp, peeled and deveined, tails removed (ask for easy-peels at seafood counter of market)

Salt and freshly ground black pepper, to taste

4 twelve-inch flour tortillas

1/2 pound shredded pepper Jack cheese (2 cups)

Make the guacamole: Cut avocados all the way around with a sharp knife. Scoop out pit with a spoon, then spoon avocado flesh away from skin into a food processor. Add lime juice, salt, sour cream, and chipotles in adobo. Pulse guacamole until smooth. Transfer to a serving bowl.

Heat a 12-inch nonstick skillet over medium-high heat. Brown chorizo 2 to 3 minutes, then remove from pan. Add evoo and garlic, then shrimp. Season shrimp with salt and pepper, and cook shrimp until pink, 2 or 3 minutes. Transfer shrimp to a cutting board and coarsely chop. Add a drizzle of oil to the pan, then a tortilla. Cook tortilla 30 seconds, then turn. Cover half of the tortilla with a couple handfuls of cheese. Arrange a layer of chorizo and shrimp over the cheese, and fold tortilla over. Press down gently with a spatula and cook tortilla a minute or so on each side to melt cheese, and crisp. Remove quesadilla to large cutting board and repeat with remaining ingredients. Cut each quesadilla into 5 wedges and transfer to plates with your spatula. Top wedges of quesadillas with liberal amounts of smoky guacamole.

GREAT DATES ROMANTIC MENUS FOR TWO

Serves 2

SEVEN SAMURAI, PLUS 2

1

PASSPORT TO JAPAN:
BENTO BOXES

EDAMAME

GYOZA WITH DIPPING SAUCE

SHORT-GRAIN RICE

TERIYAKI BEEF AND SCALLIONS

John and his best friend, Eric, are odd—that's why we, Keiko (Eric's wife) and I, love them so. They call each other Bob. Bob lives in LA. The other Bob lives in NYC. Though miles apart, these two men are as close as the last great sumo match. Keiko is, as her name might give away, Japanese. The at-home bento boxes were John's idea, the gyoza are made from her recipe, and I did the rest. It's way easier than the ingredient list looks. Plus, with leftovers, you can have an Asian twist on dinner later in the week.

The four of us also share a deep love of movies. You could easily catch either couple dining on these bentos in the middle of the living room floor, bare-footed, watching Seven Samurai. Considering the time change, you could, in theory, catch the same great movie and us twice in the same night. Itadakimasu! Good eating!

BENTO BOXES

edamame, gyoza with dipping sauce, short-grain rice, and teriyaki beef and scallions

TIP

A Gyoza Alternative: Japanese Pot Stickers

•

Two tablespoons vegetable oil
One package Japanese pot stickers, frozen
1 cup shredded cabbage

•

Preheat a medium skillet over medium-high heat, and coat with vegetable oil. Set pot stickers into hot oil, and brown for 1 or 2 minutes undisturbed. Add 1 cup of water. Cover and steam for 3 to 5 minutes. Remove to bed of shredded cabbage and serve with dipping sauce, next page. Allow about 5 to 6 pot stickers per person.

Gyoza, Rice, and Edamame

3/4 cup short-grain rice

2 cups edamame (soybeans) (from the frozen vegetables section of large markets)

Coarse salt and freshly ground black pepper, to taste

1 & 1/2 cups shredded Napa cabbage, plus 1 large whole leaf

1/4 pound ground pork

1/4 cup (300 count) baby shrimp (a handful), chopped

1 tablespoon sake, Mirin may be substituted (a splash)

1 inch fresh gingerroot, minced

1 scallion, finely chopped

1 tablespoon tamari (dark aged soy) (available on Asian food aisle of market)

12 won ton wrappers

ROMANTIC MENUS FOR TWO

GREAT DATES

105

Beef

2 fillet of beef steaks, 1 inch thick (6 ounces each)

1 teaspoon steak seasoning or salt and freshly ground black pepper

1/3 cup teriyaki sauce or 1/4 cup tamari dark aged soy, mixed with 2 tablespoons dry sherry

1 tablespoon light oil (wok, peanut or vegetable oil)

4 scallions, chopped on an angle into 1-inch pieces

Dipping Sauce

3 tablespoons tamari (eyeball it)

1 teaspoon hot sweet mustard (from Asian foods aisle), or other prepared mustard

2 teaspoons rice wine or white vinegar

Place 2 pots of water on to boil: One medium saucepan with 1 & 1/2 cups of water in it, one pasta pot with a few inches of water in it. Cover both pots and bring all the water to a boil.

When the saucepan with 1 & 1/2 cups of water comes to a boil, stir in rice and return water to a boil. Reduce heat to simmer. Place a colander over the pot and add the edamame to it. Place the pot cover over the edamame, nesting it in the colander.

TIP

To make your own bento boxes line 2 shallow boxes (about 8" x 11") with pretty contact paper. If you want to turn this meal into a funky once-a-week/month tradition, change the main course to fun hand rolls and simple sushi pieces, for example. Yummo!

Steam the edamame 5 minutes, then remove them to 2 small bowls, salt them and cover bowls with plastic or aluminum foil to keep warm. Set colander aside and return pot lid to rice, stirring rice before replacing the lid.

TIP

Warm or cold sake, leftover from cooking, is the perfect beverage, and chilled navel oranges or tangerines make a refreshing end to this meal.

While the edamame are steaming, make the gyoza: Add 1/2 cup (a couple handfuls) cabbage to the second pot of water. Blanch the shredded cabbage 1 minute and remove with a spider or tongs to paper towels to drain and cool. Chop shredded blanched cabbage. Combine pork, chopped shrimp, sake, ginger, scallion, tamari, a few grinds fresh black pepper, and the cooled, chopped cabbage in a bowl. Place 2 teaspoons of filling onto each won ton wrapper. Wet your fingertips to help seal them. The gyoza should look like small half moons.

Place a whole cabbage leaf into the bottom of the colander. The leaf will prevent the dumplings from sticking to the colander. Arrange dumplings on cabbage leaf in colander and steam over second, larger pot of simmering water. Cover and steam, 10 to 12 minutes. While you are working on this, go back and forth with the edamame as necessary per above directions.

While the dumplings cook, make the steaks: Slice them thinly across the grain. Toss with seasoning and teriyaki or tamari and sherry. Heat a nonstick skillet over high heat. Add oil and the meat, and stir-fry. When meat browns at edges, add scallions and cook 2 minutes more, stirring frequently.

Use remaining raw shredded cabbage as a bed to serve your dumplings on. Plate all of your items on little dishes and in small bowls and fit them into your boxes.

Mix a dipping sauce of tamari, mustard, and vinegar for the gyoza and set out alongside dumplings.

GREAT DATES ROMANTIC MENUS FOR TWO

107

30 MINUTE MEALS

MENU

Serves 2

MEAT AND POTATOES À DEUX

1

•

CHÂTEAUBRIAND FOR 2
IN 30:

TOURNEDOS WITH MUSHROOM CAPS

RED WINE SAUCE

DUCHESS-STYLE POTATOES

STEAMED BROCCOLI SPEARS

2

•

BLACK-AND-WHITE
ICE CREAM SANDWICHES

CHÂTEAUBRIAND FOR 2 IN 30:

tournedos with mushroom caps, red wine sauce,
   duchess-style potatoes, steamed broccoli spears

Potatoes

1 pound russet potatoes (2 medium-large potatoes)

Salt and freshly ground black pepper, to taste

2 egg yolks

2 tablespoons butter

2 tablespoons grated cheese, such as Parmesan

2 teaspoons extra-virgin olive oil (evoo)

Broccoli

2 clusters of broccoli tops, cut into spears, or 1 pound of broccolini, trimmed

Tournedos

1/2 tablespoon butter

1 tablespoon extra-virgin olive oil (evoo)

2 large stuffing mushroom caps, wiped with damp towel, stems removed

2 each, 1-inch thick beef fillets

Salt and freshly ground black pepper, to taste

Sauce

1 tablespoon butter

1 tablespoon flour

1/2 cup dry red wine

1/2 cup beef stock

Preheat oven to 450°F.

Make the potatoes: Peel and cut potatoes into chunks. Boil them until tender in salted water, about 10 minutes. Mix a little cooking water into 1 beaten egg yolk. Drain potatoes and transfer to food processor. Add egg yolk mixture, butter, and cheese. Process until smooth and add salt to taste. Scrape potatoes into a pastry bag or a cone made from rolled up waxed or parchment paper, a disposable alternative to a pastry bag.

Pipe potatoes into conical shapes on a nonstick cookie sheet or greased baking sheet.

Make a wash: Beat the remaining egg yolk with evoo and brush potatoes with wash. Bake potatoes 10 minutes, until golden.

While the potatoes cook, steam the broccoli and make the tournedos.

Steam broccoli in 1 inch of water, covered, 3 minutes. Remove from heat. Drain, but leave covered in pan for another 5 minutes. The broccoli will continue to cook, but not lose all of its color.

Make the tournedos: In a small skillet, heat butter and evoo over medium-high heat. Cook mushroom caps 3 or 4 minutes until just golden; turn them and set to sides of pan. Season meat with salt and pepper and add to skillet. Cook 3 minutes on each side for medium-rare, 5 minutes on each side for medium-well. Remove steaks and caps from the pan and cover with a loose foil tent to keep warm and let juices distribute. Make the sauce: Add butter and flour to the pan, cook for a few minutes, and whisk in wine. Scrape up drippings, reduce wine for half a minute, then whisk in a little beef stock. Thicken sauce another half minute, then remove from heat.

To serve, top each steak with a mushroom cap and pour a little sauce down over the top. Serve the potato cones and broccoli tops alongside. Makes a dinner fit for a king and a queen.

black-and-white ICE CREAM sandwiches

1/2 pint fudge swirl **ice cream**
4 three-inch chocolate cookies **or thin chocolate brownie bars (from baked goods section of the market)**
1/2 cup chopped walnuts

Place a large scoop of ice cream between 2 cookies or thin brownies and squish the ice cream out to the edges. Repeat with remaining ice cream and cookies. Roll the ice cream sandwiches in chopped walnuts and serve.

30
MINUTE
MEALS

MENU

Serves 2

UPTOWN BURGER AND FRIES

1
•

PORTOBELLO MUSHROOM
"FRIES"

2
•

SIRLOIN BOURGUIGNONNE
BURGERS

3
•

MIXED GREENS WITH
TARRAGON VINAIGRETTE

PORTOBELLO mushroom "fries"

3 large portobello mushroom caps

1/4 cup extra-virgin olive oil (evoo), plus more for drizzling

Steak seasoning blend, such as Montreal Seasoning by McCormick, or coarse salt and freshly ground black pepper, to taste

2 eggs, beaten

1/4 cup fresh flat-leaf parsley, chopped

1 cup Italian bread crumbs

1/2 cup shredded or grated Parmesan cheese

Preheat a grill pan over medium-high to high heat.

Scrape the gills off the underside of the portobello mushroom caps with a spoon. Brush caps gently with a damp cloth to clean. Drizzle caps with evoo to keep from sticking to the grill pan, and season the caps with steak seasoning or salt and pepper.

Grill mushrooms, 3 or 4 minutes on each side under a loose aluminum foil tent until just tender. Remove from heat and cool, 5 minutes.

Slice grilled caps into 1/2-inch strips. Turn strips in beaten egg, then coat in a mixture of parsley, bread crumbs, and cheese. Cook "fries" over medium-high heat in enough evoo to coat a nonstick skillet with a thin layer, about 1/4 cup. "Fries" will brown in 2 or 3 minutes on each side.

sirloin bourguignonne BURGERS

3/4 to 1 pound ground sirloin

1/4 cup red Burgundy

2 tablespoons fresh thyme, chopped

1 shallot, finely chopped

2 teaspoons steak seasoning blend, such as Montreal Seasoning by McCormick, or salt and freshly ground black pepper, to taste

Extra-virgin olive oil (evoo), for drizzling

2 crusty Kaiser rolls, split and toasted

1/4 pound (1/2-inch slice) mousse-style pâté (available near specialty cheeses in large markets)

4 cornichon pickles or baby gherkins, thinly sliced lengthwise

4 pieces red leaf lettuce

Grainy mustard or Dijon-style mustard, to spread on buns

Preheat a grill pan or grill to medium-high heat. If using a charcoal grill, prepare coals.

Make the burgers: Combine ground sirloin with wine, thyme, shallot, and steak seasoning or salt and pepper. Form meat into 2 large patties, 1 to 1 & 1/2 inches thick. Drizzle patties with evoo to keep them from sticking to grill or grill pan. Cook patties 5 minutes on each side for medium-rare, 8 minutes on each side for medium-well.

Toast rolls under a hot broiler or in toaster oven. Spread mousse pâté on the bun bottoms. Top with burger, cornichons, and red leaf lettuce. Spread the bun tops with mustard and set on burgers.

MIXED GREENS with tarragon vinaigrette

5 ounces (half a 10-ounce sack) mixed baby greens

2 scallions, thinly sliced on an angle

<u>Vinaigrette</u>

2 tablespoons fresh tarragon leaves, chopped

1/2 teaspoon grainy or Dijon-style mustard

2 teaspoons white wine vinegar (2 splashes)

2 tablespoons extra-virgin olive oil (evoo) (eyeball it)

Salt and freshly ground black pepper, to taste

Place greens and scallions in a medium bowl. Whisk tarragon, mustard, and vinegar together and add evoo in a slow stream while whisking. Pour dressing on greens and toss with tongs. Season salad with salt and pepper, to taste.

ROMANTIC MENUS FOR TWO

GREAT DATES

113

30 MINUTE MEALS

MENU

Serves 2

LIFE IS A BOWL OF CHERRIES

1

PORK CHOPS WITH
BRANDIED CHERRY SAUCE

2

ZUCCHINI WITH WALNUTS

3

BLACK CHERRY ICE CREAM WITH
CHOCOLATE SAUCE

PORK CHOPS with brandied cherry sauce and ZUCCHINI with walnuts

20 to 24 fresh Bing cherries or 1 cup canned, drained black pitted cherries in natural juices

2 rounded teaspoonfuls sugar (for fresh cherries only)

2 large boneless center-cut pork chops, 1 to 1 & 1/2 inches thick

Salt and freshly ground black pepper, to taste

2 tablespoons extra-virgin olive oil (evoo) (twice around the pan)

1 large shallot, finely chopped

3 ounces (2 shots) brandy

1/2 cup chicken stock

1 tablespoon butter, cut into pieces

2 tablespoons fresh mint, finely chopped

Zucchini

2 ounces (1/4 cup) chopped walnuts (found in small sacks on baking aisle)

1 tablespoon extra-virgin olive oil (evoo) (once around the pan)

1 tablespoon butter, cut into small pieces

1 medium zucchini, sliced into 1/4-inch-thick disks

1/4 teaspoon freshly grated nutmeg, or a pinch of ground

Salt and freshly ground black pepper, to taste

Preheat oven to 375°F.

Pull stems off clean, fresh cherries. Pop pits away from cherries by placing the flat of your kitchen knife on top of a cherry or two at a time and giving the cherry a whack with the heel of your hand, just like cracking garlic from its skin. Discard pits and place fruit in a small bowl. Sugar cherries and let stand until ready to cook.

Heat an ovenproof skillet over medium-high to high heat. If you don't have an ovenproof skillet, cover the handle of a rubber-handled pan with aluminum foil.

Season chops with salt and pepper. Add 1 tablespoon evoo, once around the pan, to hot skillet. Place chops in skillet and sear meat on both sides to caramelize. Place a loose foil tent over the pan and transfer the chops to oven to finish off, 7 or 8 minutes, until meat is firm to touch, but not tough.

While chops are in oven, make the zucchini: Place a second skillet over medium-high heat. Toast nuts a minute or two, shaking pan frequently. Remove nuts to cool and

add evoo, and butter. Add zucchini, season with nutmeg, salt, and pepper, and cook
until tender, tossing occasionally, 6 or 7 minutes.

Remove meat from oven and transfer to dinner plates. Cover chops with foil to keep
warm. Place chop skillet back on stove over medium heat. Add 1 tablespoon evoo.
Add shallots and sauté, 1 to 2 minutes. Add cherries and warm through. Add brandy
by removing the pan off the burner to add the alcohol, then flame the pan. Burn off
alcohol for 1 minute, then add stock. Reduce stock a minute, then add butter in small
pieces. Toss sauce to combine and sprinkle in mint. Pour sauce down over chops
and serve the zucchini with a generous topping of toasted walnuts alongside. Makes
2 yummy-in-the-tummy BIG servings.

BLACK CHERRY ICE CREAM
with chocolate sauce

1 pint black cherry ice cream
2 ounces cherry liqueur, **such as Kirsch (optional)**
1/4 cup chocolate sauce

Place 2 scoops black cherry ice cream in each of 2 cocktail glasses. Top with a splash of
cherry liqueur, if desired, and a drizzle of chocolate sauce.

Serves 2

TV DINNER FOR 2

1

TV DINNER:

SALISBURY STEAK WITH
WILD MUSHROOM GRAVY

SMASHED POTATOES WITH
GARLIC & HERB CHEESE AND CHIVES

CREAMED SPINACH

2

QUICK GINGER PEACH COBBLER

This meal is a tribute dinner that John and I wrote in honor of our friend and inspiration, chef Jon Young, of Kitch'n on Roscoe in Chicago. Jon is our age and has this too-groovy restaurant that serves upscale versions of familiar foods. He makes Twinkie tiramisu and psychedelic TV dinners. This gourmet-made-everyday Salisbury steak dinner is a winner. Enjoy it while watching Starsky & Hutch reruns or Shaft videos with someone you love.

quick ginger PEACH COBBLER

1 can (14 & 1/2 ounces) sliced peaches in juice, drained

1 inch fresh gingerroot, minced, or 1/2 teaspoon ground ginger

1 tablespoon softened butter

2 tablespoons brown sugar

1/2 cup granola cereal with raisins and nuts

1 egg white, beaten

Store-bought real whipped cream in spray canister (from dairy aisle)

Preheat oven to 400°F.

Mix drained peaches with ginger. Place sliced peaches in small ovenproof bowls.

Combine butter and sugar with a fork, then mix with granola. Fold in beaten egg white.

Mound the topping on top of the peaches. Place dishes on a small baking sheet and bake, 10 to 12 minutes. Remove and cool cobbler while you enjoy dinner.

After dinner, serve warm cobbler with whipped cream.

TV DINNER: salisbury steak with wild mushroom gravy, smashed potatoes with garlic & herb cheese and chives, creamed spinach

Potatoes

1 pound russet potatoes (2 large potatoes), peeled and chunked

Salt and freshly ground black pepper, to taste

1/4 cup half-and-half or cream (eyeball it)

3 ounces (1/3 cup or half of one small container), garlic and herb cheese, such as Boursin

2 tablespoons chopped chives (6 blades), or 1 scallion, thinly sliced

Meat and Gravy

3/4 pound ground beef sirloin

2 teaspoons Worcestershire sauce (eyeball it)

1/2 small onion, finely chopped

1 teaspoon steak seasoning blend, such as Montreal Seasoning by McCormick, or coarse salt and freshly ground black pepper, to taste

Extra-virgin olive oil (evoo), 3 tablespoons (3 times around the pan)

1 tablespoon butter

6 crimini or baby portobello mushrooms, sliced

6 shiitake mushrooms, chopped

Salt and freshly ground black pepper, to taste

1 tablespoon flour

1/2 cup beef stock

Spinach

1 box (10 ounces) chopped spinach, defrosted in microwave

1 tablespoon butter, cut into pieces

1/4 cup half-and-half or heavy cream

Salt and freshly ground black pepper, to taste

Start the potatoes: Place them in a pot with water. Cover pot, bring to a boil and lightly salt. Leave uncovered and simmer at rolling boil until tender, 8 to 10 minutes.

While potatoes cook, make the steaks: Combine meat, Worcestershire, onion, and steak seasoning, or salt and pepper. Form 2 large, oval patties, 1 inch thick.

Preheat a large nonstick skillet over medium-high heat. Add a tablespoon of evoo and meat patties to hot pan. Cook 6 minutes on each side until meat is evenly caramelized on the outside and juices run clear. Remove meat and cover with loose aluminum foil to keep warm. Add 1 more tablespoon evoo and the butter to the pan, then the mushrooms. Season with salt and pepper, and sauté until tender, 3 to 5 minutes.

While mushrooms cook, make the spinach: To a small skillet, add butter and cream and heat to a bubble over moderate heat. Add the defrosted and "dried" spinach and salt and pepper. Cook until spinach thickens with cream, 3 to 5 minutes.

To mushrooms, add a sprinkle of flour to the pan and cook 2 minutes more. Whisk in stock and thicken 1 minute.

While sauce thickens, drain potatoes and return them to hot pot. Smash potatoes with a little half-and-half or cream and garlic and herb cheese. Smash and incorporate chives. Add salt and pepper to taste.

To serve, pour gravy over steak. Serve potatoes and creamed spinach alongside the steaks. Now that's a TV dinner, DELUXE!

ROMANTIC MENUS FOR TWO

GREAT DATES

30
MINUTE
MEALS

MENU

Serves 2

EXPRESS LANE DINNER DATE— 10 ITEMS OR LESS

1

ROSEMARY
CHICKEN BREASTS

2

BROWN BUTTER AND
BALSAMIC RAVIOLI

3

TOMATO AND ONION SALAD

Even when you shop and cook together, it's still a date. This menu is great for busy couples: 3 courses from 10 items, so you can hit the express lane at your market. The menu is especially romantic to me because it combines recipes of John's and mine. We eat this meal often.

rosemary chicken BREASTS, brown butter and balsamic RAVIOLI, TOMATO AND ONION salad

Chicken

2 pieces (6 to 8 ounces each) boneless, skinless chicken breasts

1 tablespoon balsamic vinegar, just enough to coat chicken lightly (eyeball it)

2 tablespoons extra-virgin olive oil (evoo)

2 stems rosemary, stripped of leaves and chopped (1 tablespoon)

Salt and coarsely ground black pepper, to taste

2 cloves garlic, cracked away from skin with a whack against the flat of a knife

Ravioli

Salt and freshly ground black pepper, to taste

1 package (12 to 16 ounces) fresh ravioli, any flavor filling

3 tablespoons butter, cut into small pieces

2 tablespoons balsamic vinegar

2 handfuls grated Parmigiano Reggiano cheese

1/4 cup fresh flat-leaf parsley, chopped (a couple handfuls)

Salad

4 vine-ripe tomatoes, seeded and chopped

1/2 small white onion, thinly sliced

1/4 cup flat leaf parsley, chopped (a couple handfuls)

2 tablespoons extra-virgin olive oil (evoo) (eyeball it)

Salt and freshly ground black pepper, to taste

Marinate the chicken: Coat chicken in balsamic vinegar, then olive oil. Season chicken with rosemary, salt, and pepper and let stand, 10 minutes.

Start the ravioli: Bring a large pot of water to a boil. Salt water and drop ravioli in water. Cook 6 to 8 minutes or until raviolis expand and float to top of water and are al dente. Drain.

ROMANTIC MENUS FOR TWO

GREAT DATES

121

Heat a medium nonstick skillet over medium-high heat. Add chicken breasts and cracked garlic to the pan. Cook chicken, 10 to 12 minutes, or until juices run clear, turning occasionally. The balsamic vinegar will produce a deep brown, sweet finish on the chicken as it cooks.

When the chicken has cooked midway, 5 or 6 minutes, start to prepare butter for ravioli:

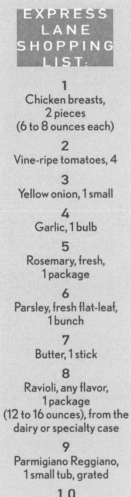

EXPRESS LANE SHOPPING LIST:

1
Chicken breasts,
2 pieces
(6 to 8 ounces each)

2
Vine-ripe tomatoes, 4

3
Yellow onion, 1 small

4
Garlic, 1 bulb

5
Rosemary, fresh,
1 package

6
Parsley, fresh flat-leaf,
1 bunch

7
Butter, 1 stick

8
Ravioli, any flavor,
1 package
(12 to 16 ounces), from the
dairy or specialty case

9
Parmigiano Reggiano,
1 small tub, grated

1 0
Balsamic vinegar

•
Pantry ingredients:
Extra-virgin olive oil (evoo)
Salt and fresh black
pepper

To a cold skillet, add butter and turn on moderate heat. Let the butter brown. If you start with a cold pan, the butter should be lightly browned by the time it comes to a bubble.

When the butter for the ravioli has browned, add cooked ravioli to the pan and turn in butter to heat through. Add balsamic vinegar to the ravioli and cook a minute or two longer to reduce the vinegar and glaze the ravioli. The vinegar will become thick and syruplike. Add cheese, parsley, salt, and pepper to the pasta and remove the pan from the heat.

Make the salad: Combine the tomatoes, onions, parsley, evoo, salt, and pepper. Toss to coat salad evenly with oil and to mix in salt and pepper. Adjust seasonings.

Slice cooked chicken on an angle and serve with Ravioli and Tomato and Onion Salad alongside.

THE BIG GAME

MENUS FOR SPORTS FANS

I love sports! I love other people who love sports! I love the passion, ferocity, devotion, anguish—the pure drama of being a sports fan! All of this drama can make one weak from hunger. Pass the food! Lots of it! Baseball, football, hockey, basketball, soccer, even Monopoly: when there is a serious game on, you need serious food. Whether you're an armchair quarterback, tailgater or into a serious game of rummy or bridge, here are the menus that will score big!

RACHAEL RAY 30-MINUTE MEALS
gettogethers

Serves 8

3 CHEERS
FOR CHILI!

1
•

CHILI MAC

2
•

MEXICAN SUPREME PIZZAS

3
•

SPICY POPCORN

CHILI mac

- **2 pounds** ground sirloin
- **2 tablespoons extra-virgin** olive oil **(evoo) (twice around the pan in a slow stream)**
- **1 sweet** onion, **chopped**
- **2** jalapeño peppers, **seeded and chopped**
- **4 cloves** garlic, **chopped**
- **3 tablespoons** dark chili powder **(1 & 1/2 palmfuls)**
- **2 tablespoons** cumin **(a palmful)**
- **2 tablespoons** cayenne pepper sauce **(such as Frank's Red Hot)**
- **Coarse** salt, **to taste**
- **1 cup** beer **or beef broth**
- **1 can (28 ounces)** diced tomatoes **in juice**
- **1 can (14 ounces)** crushed tomatoes
- **1 pound** corkscrew shaped pasta **with lines or elbows with lines, cooked to al dente and drained**
- **Chopped** scallions, **for garnish**

In a big, deep pot, brown beef in evoo over medium-high heat. Add onions, peppers, and garlic. Season meat mixture with chili powder, cumin, cayenne, and salt. Cook together 5 minutes, stir in beer or broth and reduce liquid by half, 2 minutes. Stir in tomatoes and simmer.

Add hot pasta to chili pot and stir to coat pasta evenly. Remove from heat and garnish big bowlfuls of chili mac with chopped scallions.

THE BIG GAME MENUS FOR SPORTS FANS

125

mexican supreme PIZZAS

1 small red bell pepper, **seeded and diced**

1 small onion, **chopped**

A handful of cilantro, **chopped**

2 tablespoons sliced salad olives with pimiento, **drained**

4 mushroom caps, **thinly sliced**

2 store-bought thin-crust pizza shells **(such as Boboli brand)**

1 cup store-bought salsa, **any variety (I like smoky chipotle salsa)**

1 brick (8 ounces) smoked cheddar **cheese, shredded**

1/2 pound chorizo sausage, **casing removed and thinly sliced**

1 cup shredded Monterey Jack **cheese (found on dairy aisle)**

Preheat oven to 425°F.

Combine first 5 ingredients in a bowl and mix. Place pizza crusts on 2 cookie sheets or perforated pizza pans. Spread 1/2 cup salsa on each pizza and top with smoked cheese. Top each pie with half the veggie blend and half of the chorizo. Top with the remaining Monterey Jack and bake. Bake pizzas 10 minutes, until cheese is golden and toppings tender. Cut pizzas into squares and serve.

spicy POPCORN

2 tablespoons vegetable oil

1 cup popping corn kernels

2 tablespoons melted butter

1/2 teaspoon sweet paprika

1 teaspoon salt

1/2 teaspoon garlic powder

1 teaspoon cumin

1/4 teaspoon cayenne pepper

Heat oil in a deep pot with a cover over medium-high heat. Add corn. Cover pot and pop the corn, shaking pan often. Remove from heat. Drizzle with melted butter. Combine spices in a small dish and sprinkle the blend over hot popcorn. Serve.

30 MINUTE MEALS

MENU

Serves 4

COUCH COACH'S NACHOS

1
•

SUPER NACHOS:

MIXED CHIPS

PICO DE GALLO SALSA

BEEF AND BEANS TOPPING

CHEESE SAUCE

2
•

MEXICAN CARAMEL
SUNDAES

SUPER NACHOS

2 bags corn tortilla chips in 2 colors or different flavors, such as blue corn, red corn, yellow corn, lime-flavored, chili-flavored, or black bean chips—pick 2 favorites

Pico de Gallo Salsa

4 vine-ripe tomatoes, seeded and chopped

1 or 2 jalapeño peppers, seeded and finely chopped, for medium to hot heat level

1 small white onion, chopped

1/4 cup cilantro leaves or parsley, finely chopped (2 handfuls)

Salt, to taste

Beef and Beans Topping

1 tablespoon extra-virgin olive oil (evoo)

2 cloves garlic, chopped

1 small onion, chopped

1 jalapeño or Serrano pepper, seeded and chopped

1 pound ground sirloin

1 teaspoon salt

1 & 1/2 teaspoons dark chili powder

1 & 1/2 teaspoons cumin (half palmful)

2 teaspoons to 1 tablespoon cayenne pepper sauce (such as Frank's Red Hot) for medium to hot heat level

1 can (15 ounces) black beans, drained

Cheese Sauce

2 tablespoons butter

2 tablespoons flour

2 cups milk

2 & 1/2 cups (about 3/4 pound) pepper Jack cheese, shredded

Arrange a mixture of 2 varieties of corn chips on a very large platter, or use your broiler pan as a platter.

Combine salsa ingredients in a bowl and set aside for flavors to blend.

Make the beef and beans topping: Heat a medium nonstick skillet over medium-high heat. Add evoo, garlic, onion, and jalapeño to the pan and sauté, 2 minutes; add meat and crumble with a wooden spoon. Season meat with salt, chili powder, cumin,

THE BIG GAME MENUS FOR SPORTS FANS

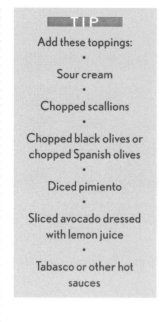

TIP

Add these toppings:

•

Sour cream

•

Chopped scallions

•

Chopped black olives or chopped Spanish olives

•

Diced pimiento

•

Sliced avocado dressed with lemon juice

•

Tabasco or other hot sauces

and cayenne pepper sauce. Cook meat 5 minutes, then stir in beans and reduce heat to low.

Make the cheese sauce: In a medium saucepan, melt butter and add flour to it. Cook flour and butter a minute or two over moderate heat, then whisk in milk. When milk comes to a bubble, stir in cheese with a wooden spoon. Remove cheese sauce from the heat.

Pour cheese sauce evenly over the massive spread of chips and top evenly with beef and beans and the Pico de Gallo Salsa. ÜBER NACHOS! Serve immediately as is or garnish with your choice of additional toppings from the list.

mexican caramel SUNDAES

8 ounces store-bought caramel sauce **for ice cream**

1/4 teaspoon cayenne pepper

1 teaspoon cinnamon

4 eight-inch flour tortillas

2 tablespoons melted butter

4 teaspoons sugar

2 pints dulce de leche caramel ice cream **or caramel swirl ice cream**

Store-bought real whipped cream **in a spray can**

1/2 cup (4 ounces) Spanish peanuts

Preheat oven to 400°F.

In a small saucepan, warm caramel sauce over low heat and season with cayenne pepper and 1/2 teaspoon cinnamon. Place tortillas on a cookie sheet and brush liberally with melted butter. Sprinkle each tortilla with sugar and a pinch of cinnamon and bake until crispy and sugar has melted onto tortillas, 5 minutes. Remove tortillas from oven and cut into wedges. Arrange the pieces of 1 tortilla in each sundae dish or on a dessert plate. Top with 2 large scoops ice cream. Drizzle the warm spicy caramel sauce over each sundae using a spatula or wooden spoon. Top each sundae with whipped cream swirls and Spanish peanuts. Makes 4 BIG sundaes.

30 MINUTE MEALS

MENU

Serves 4

BOARD GAME
NIGHT MUNCHIES

1
•

MINI SANDWICH BUFFET:

MINI GRILLED CHEESE
AND TOMATO

MINI RACHAELS
(SMOKED TURKEY RUEBENS)

MINI SPICY PATTY MELTS

MINI SANDWICH BUFFET:

mini grilled cheese and tomato, mini rachaels, and mini spicy patty melts

For 24 mini sandwiches

2 tablespoons vegetable oil (eyeball it)

4 tablespoons butter, cut into pieces

Mini Grilled Cheese and Tomato

16 slices mini pumpernickel bread

1/4 pound thinly sliced Swiss cheese

2 plum tomatoes, sliced

Salt and freshly ground black pepper, to taste

2 tablespoons chopped chives or 2 scallions, chopped

Mini Rachaels

16 slices mini rye bread

1/2 cup sweet red pepper relish

1 pound smoked turkey, thinly sliced

1 pound sauerkraut, rinsed and drained

1/3 pound thinly sliced sharp cheddar cheese

Mini Spicy Patty Melts

1 pound ground sirloin

2 teaspoons Worcestershire sauce (several drops)

1/2 small onion, finely chopped

1 teaspoon steak seasoning blend, such as Montreal Seasoning by McCormick or salt and fresh black pepper

1 tablespoon vegetable oil (once around the pan)

16 slices mini rye bread

1/4 pound thinly sliced Swiss cheese

Preheat oven to 250°F.

Preheat a large griddle or large nonstick skillet over medium heat.

To a small pot over medium-low heat add vegetable oil. Add butter and melt it into the oil. Keep a pastry brush handy on a spoon rest or small plate.

Make the Mini Grilled Cheese and Tomato Sandwiches: Lay out 8 slices of mini pumpernickel bread. Cut Swiss cheese slices into pieces that will fit bread. Layer cheese and sliced tomatoes on bread. Season with salt, pepper, and chives and place another layer of cheese on tomatoes. Top sandwiches with another slice of bread. Brush griddle or skillet liberally with oil and butter. Grill and toast sandwiches, 2 or 3 minutes on each side. Transfer grilled sandwiches to warm oven. Wipe griddle or skillet clean.

Make the Mini Rachaels: Lay out 8 slices of rye bread. Dot bread with teaspoonfuls of red pepper relish. Top with even amounts of smoked turkey, sauerkraut, and cheese. Top cheese with remaining slices of bread. Brush griddle or skillet with oil-and-butter mixture. Grill and toast sandwiches, 2 or 3 minutes on each side. Transfer sandwiches to a cookie sheet and place in oven to keep warm. Wipe off griddle or skillet.

Make the Patty Melts: Mix beef, Worcestershire, onion, and seasoning, or salt and pepper. Form 8 small patties. Raise heat to medium-high. Fry patties in vegetable oil on griddle or skillet 2 or 3 minutes on each side. Place patties on 8 rye bread bottoms and wipe griddle or skillet clean. Top patties with cheese and another slice of bread. Reduce heat on griddle or skillet back to medium and brush with oil and butter. Grill sandwiches 2 or 3 minutes on each side until toasted.

Remove Mini Rachael's and Grilled Cheese and Tomato Sandwiches from the warm oven. Pass trays of sandwiches with mini pickles and mini pretzels. Mini candies and cookies treat your sweet tooth.

TIP

Suggested accompaniments: mini pickles and mini pretzels.

·

Suggested dessert: Retro candies such as Dots, Good 'n Plenty, Whoppers, etc. and Pepperidge Farm brand Chess Men butter cookies.

THE BIG GAME MENUS FOR SPORTS FANS

133

30 MINUTE MEALS

MENU

Serves 6

A TRADITIONALIST'S TAILGATE

1

SPICY DOUBLE-DIPPED CHICKEN

2

MOM'S POTATO SALAD WITH PIMIENTO AND PEAS

3

CARROT RAISIN SALAD

spicy double-dipped CHICKEN

Vegetable oil, for frying

3 shallow dishes or disposable pie tins (optional, for easy clean-up)

1 & 1/2 cups flour

1 teaspoon paprika (1/3 palmful)

1 teaspoon poultry seasoning

1/4 teaspoon cayenne pepper (eyeball it)

1/4 teaspoon allspice (eyeball it)

1 cup buttermilk

1 pound boneless, skinless chicken thighs

1 & 1/2 pounds chicken breast tenderloins

Salt and freshly ground black pepper, to taste

Heat 1 & 1/2 inches vegetable oil in a deep skillet over medium-high heat. To test if the oil is hot enough, drop a cube of bread in it and count to 40; the bread should be brown by 40.

Set out 3 shallow dishes or disposable pie tins. Mix flour with paprika, poultry seasoning, cayenne, and allspice. Divide seasoned flour between 2 tins or dishes. Pour buttermilk into a third tin or dish. Line up tins or dishes as such: flour, buttermilk, flour.

Season chicken with salt and pepper. Coat chicken pieces in flour, then buttermilk, then a second coating of flour. Discard tins.

Fry chicken, 6 minutes on each side, until deep golden brown and firm. Drain chicken on paper bags and cool before packing up for picnic basket.

mom's POTATO SALAD

with pimiento and peas

The onion juice is what makes this salad so good.

2 & 1/2 pounds white thin-skinned potatoes, peeled and diced
Salt and freshly ground black pepper, to taste
2 tablespoons white vinegar or cider vinegar
1 jar (6 ounces) sliced pimiento, drained and chopped
1 cup frozen sweet peas
1 small white onion, peeled and left whole
1/2 cup mayonnaise or reduced-fat mayo (just enough to bind salad)

Boil potatoes in salted water for 12 minutes, until fork-tender. Drain and return potatoes to hot pot to dry them. Sprinkle potatoes with vinegar. Transfer potatoes to a bowl and let them cool.

When potatoes have cooled, add pimiento and peas to the bowl. Using a handheld grater, grate onion over potatoes. Add mayonnaise to bind. Season potato salad with salt and pepper, to taste. Transfer to plastic servingware and pack up for your picnic. Keep this salad in your cooler with beverages or chill until ready to travel.

CARROT RAISIN salad

5 to 6 cups (2 ten-ounce sacks) shredded carrots (available in produce department)
1 cup raisins (3 handfuls)
2 tablespoons poppy seeds (available on spice aisle)
Juice of 1 lemon
Juice of 2 oranges
1/2 cup light brown sugar (2 handfuls)
Salt, to taste

TIP
Slice up some watermelon wedges for a sweet, refreshing, and portable dessert.

Combine all ingredients well, using your fingers to toss and coat the carrots thoroughly. Transfer to a travel container or serving dish. As the salad sits, the raisins will plump a bit and carrots will take on citrus flavors.

30 MINUTE MEALS

MENU

Serves 8

A TAILGATE WITH GUSTO

1

MACHO GAZPACHO

2

SPITFIRE SHRIMP

3

ANTIPASTO PIE

Football's not for woosies—neither is this menu

macho GAZPACHO

2 cans (28 ounces each) diced tomatoes in purée

1/4 cup cayenne pepper sauce (such as Frank's Red Hot) for mild, use 2 tablespoons

1/2 seedless English cucumber, cut into chunks

1 small red onion, cut into chunks

2 seeded jalapeño or Serrano peppers, coarsely chopped

2 stalks celery from the heart of stalk, chunked

A handful of fresh cilantro leaves

Juice of 1 lemon or lime

Coarse salt and freshly ground black pepper, to taste

Wedges of lime or lemon, for garnish

TIP

Suggested accompaniments for this tailgate party:

•

Selections of green and black olives

•

2 bags gourmet potato chip selections, such as Terra Chips or Olive Oil Potato Chip Company brands. Try Rosemary or Black Pepper flavors.

Working in batches, combine all ingredients in a food processor and pulse-grind into a thick soup. Adjust seasonings. Pour soup into a thermos and chill until ready to serve. Serve in chilled glasses with wedges of lime or lemon for garnish. Makes 2 & 1/2 quarts (10 cups).

spitfire SHRIMP

Seasoning

Juice of 1 lime

2 ounces (1/4 cup) cayenne pepper sauce (such as Frank's Red Hot)

1 tablespoon ground cumin (half palmful)

1/2 teaspoon crushed red pepper flakes (eyeball it), and crush flakes in your hand (wash hands right away)

1 tablespoon seafood seasoning blend (such as Old Bay Seasoning)

Shrimp

4 cloves garlic, crushed and chopped

2 shallots, chopped

1 tablespoon extra-virgin olive oil (evoo) (once around the pan)

2 tablespoons butter, cut into pieces

2 pounds jumbo shrimp, peeled and deveined (ask for easy-peel raw deveined shrimp at seafood counter of market)

12 to 15 blades fresh chives, chopped, for garnish

Preheat large nonstick skillet over medium-high heat.

Make the seasoning: Combine lime juice, cayenne pepper sauce, cumin, red pepper flakes, and seafood seasoning blend.

Make the shrimp: Quickly sauté garlic and shallots in evoo and butter for 1 minute, add shrimp and cook, 3 minutes, tossing and turning frequently, until pink and firm. Dump cooked shrimp from hot pan into hot seasoning blend and toss to coat evenly. Garnish with chopped chives. Serve warm or chilled. Makes 8 servings, as a snack or first course.

THE BIG GAME MENUS FOR SPORTS FANS

ANTIPASTO pie

1 large, 12- to 14-inch round, or oval loaf of crusty, chewy bread, such as Tuscan or sesame semolina

1 jar (16 to 18 ounces) giardiniera (pickled vegetables: hot peppers, cauliflower, carrots) (available on the Italian foods aisle of market or in bulk bins near deli section with bulk olives)

1/2 pound sharp provolone cheese, deli-sliced

1 jar (14 to 16 ounces) roasted red peppers

1 can (15 ounces) quartered artichoke hearts in water, drained

1 sack (10 ounces) mixed greens (from your produce department), any variety

1/2 cup fresh flat-leaf parsley leaves (a couple handfuls)

15 to 20 leaves fresh basil, torn

Extra-virgin olive oil (evoo), for drizzling

1/3 pound Genoa salami, deli-sliced

1/3 pound sweet sopressata, deli-sliced

1/3 pound cappicola hot ham, deli sliced

1/4 red onion, thinly sliced

1 vine-ripe tomato, thinly sliced

Coarse salt and freshly ground black pepper, to taste

8 hot or sweet pickled cherry peppers

8 ten- or twelve-inch bamboo skewers

Cut the top off of loaf and hollow it out, leaving a 1/2-inch rim at edges and bottom. Pulse-grind giardiniera in a food processor into a coarse relish. Spread and press relish into the bottom of the bread shell in an even layer. Top relish with a layer of provolone slices, red pepper pieces, and artichoke hearts. Press ingredients down as you work to make room in your shell for as much antipasto as possible. Combine mixed greens, parsley, and basil in a bowl. Add a thin layer of greens on top of artichokes and drizzle with evoo. Layer in meats and remaining cheese. Top with a few more greens, onion, and tomato, and another drizzle of evoo. Season top of filled shell with salt and pepper. (Bag up unused greens and herbs for tomorrow night's salad.) Replace top of bread and wrap your GIANT, dripless antipasto-stuffed pie for travel. When you are ready to serve, spear hot or sweet cherry peppers on 10- or 12-inch bamboo skewers and space eight skewers around the bread. Cut bread into wedges, like a pie, and serve with olives and fancy potato chips. YUMMO!

Serves 6

BIG WRAP TAILGATE PARTY

1

THAI CHICKEN WRAP
WITH SPICY PEANUT SAUCE

2

MARC ANTONY'S
SCAMPI WRAP

3

MED SPREAD AND VEG WRAP

Don't let the length of these three separate ingredient lists intimidate you. This is a very simple tailgate party to pull off. If friends, family, or kids want to help, let them wrap and roll with you. This menu yields 12 BIG wraps total, 1/2 of each wrap per person is the offering.

THAI CHICKEN WRAP
with spicy peanut sauce

3 chicken breasts (6 ounces each)

1 tablespoon soy sauce

1 tablespoon vegetable oil

Salad

1/2 seedless English cucumber, peeled, halved lengthwise and thinly sliced on an angle

2 cups fresh bean spouts

1 cup shredded carrots (available in sacks in produce department)

3 scallions, sliced on an angle

12 leaves basil, chopped or torn

3 tablespoons chopped mint (4 sprigs)

1 tablespoon sesame seeds

2 teaspoons sugar

2 tablespoons rice wine vinegar or white vinegar

Salt, to taste

Sauce

1/4 cup room temperature chunky peanut butter (soften in microwave if it has been refrigerated)

2 tablespoons soy sauce

1 tablespoon rice wine vinegar or white vinegar

1/4 teaspoon cayenne pepper

2 tablespoons vegetable oil

4 twelve-inch flour tortilla wraps

TIP

To complete the menu:

•

Mixed nuts

•

Whole pieces of fruit

•

Gourmet potato chip selections, such as Terra Chips or Olive Oil Potato Chip Company brands (available in many larger markets).

•

For dessert, cut and serve store-bought brownies.

Heat grill pan over high heat. In a bowl, toss chicken with soy and oil. Grill 6 minutes on each side.

Make the salad: Combine cucumber, sprouts, carrots, scallions, basil, mint, and sesame seeds with a generous sprinkle of sugar and vinegar. Season with salt, to taste.

Make the sauce. Whisk peanut butter, soy sauce, vinegar, and cayenne together. Stream
   in vegetable oil.

Slice cooked chicken thinly on an angle. Toss with the salad.

In a very hot nonstick skillet or over a gas burner, heat tortillas 15 seconds on each side.

Pile chicken and salad in wraps and drizzle liberally with spicy peanut sauce before
   wrapping and rolling. Slice in half on an angle and serve.

marc antony's SCAMPI WRAP

Shrimp

   2 tablespoons extra-virgin olive oil (evoo) (twice around the pan)

   4 cloves garlic, crushed

   1 teaspoon red pepper flakes

   24 shrimp, peeled and deveined, tails removed (ask for easy-peel raw
      deveined shrimp at seafood counter of market)

   1 teaspoon grill seasoning blend, such as Montreal Seasoning by
      McCormick, or salt and freshly ground black pepper, to taste

Salad

   2 hearts romaine lettuce

   3 tablespoons capers

   4 anchovies fillets, chopped (optional)

   Zest and juice of 1 lemon

   2 tablespoons extra-virgin olive oil (evoo) (twice around the bowl)

   Salt and freshly ground black pepper, to taste

   4 twelve-inch spinach or sun-dried tomato-flavored flour tortilla wraps

Cook the shrimp: Heat a large skillet over medium high heat. Add evoo, garlic, and
   pepper flakes. Add shrimp and seasoning. Cook stirring frequently, 3 minutes or
   until shrimp is pink and firm. Transfer shrimp to a cutting board until cool enough to
   handle, 2 minutes. Coarsely chop shrimp and garlic. Wipe out pan.

Make the salad: Chop hearts of romaine and place in a large bowl. Add chopped
   shrimp, capers, anchovies, and lemon zest and juice. Toss salad, then add evoo, and
   retoss. Season with salt and pepper.

Blister tortillas in very hot nonstick skillet or over the open flame on a gas burner for 15
   seconds on each side to soften. Pile a quarter of the salad on each wrap. Tuck in
   sides, wrap, and roll. Repeat.

med spread and veg WRAP

4 twelve-inch spinach flour tortilla wraps

2 cups prepared hummus, any flavor

2 hearts romaine lettuce, chopped

1 cup crumbled feta cheese

1/4 cup sun-dried tomatoes, chopped

3 tablespoons chopped mint (4 sprigs)

1/2 cup fresh flat-leaf parsley leaves

1/2 cup pitted Kalamata black olives, chopped

1/4 seedless English cucumber, chopped

1/2 medium red onion, chopped

1 & 1/2 tablespoons red wine vinegar (a couple splashes)

3 tablespoons extra-virgin olive oil (evoo)

Salt and freshly ground black pepper, to taste

TIP

To transport the wraps, leave them whole. Wrap individually in waxed paper. Take a cutting board and a sharp knife with you. Cut wraps in half and pile up on the tailgate. Keep the wraps wrapped as you eat them, peeling back paper as you munch. The waxed paper will keep the wrap from dripping on you.

Warm tortillas in a nonstick skillet or over the open flame on gas burner, 15 seconds on each side, to soften. Cool to handle. Spread each wrap with 1/2 cup hummus. Toss remaining salad ingredients in a bowl and dress with vinegar, evoo, salt and pepper. Pile salad on hummus, tuck in sides of wrap and roll.

30 MINUTE MEALS

MENU

Serves 8

GOAL! FORZA ROMA BUFFET

1
•

ITALIAN-STYLE
MAC 'N CHEESE

2
•

MISS RACHAEL'S
MUFFALETTA

3
•

ESPRESSO BROWNIES

espresso BROWNIES

1 package store-bought brownie mix, **any brand, batter prepared to package directions**

3 tablespoons instant espresso **or 2 rounded tablespoons finely ground dark-roast coffee beans**

1 shot coffee liqueur **(Kahlúa) or 1 ounce coffee-flavored syrup**

Softened butter, **for pan**

Disposable 9 x 13 baking pan

Preheat oven to 425°F.

To prepared brownie mix add instant espresso or ground coffee and coffee liqueur or syrup. Butter pan and bake brownies, 22 to 25 minutes on upper rack of oven. Cut brownies into 16 bar-shaped pieces and serve warm as is or with your choice of cold milk, coffee ice cream, coffee beverages, or Italian after-dinner liqueurs.

italian-style MAC 'N CHEESE

Salt **and freshly ground black** pepper, **to taste**

1 pound ziti rigate, **penne rigate, or cavatappi (ribbed, hollow corkscrews)**

1 pound Italian bulk sweet sausage

2 tablespoons extra-virgin olive oil **(evoo)**

1 tablespoon butter

3 or 4 cloves garlic, **chopped**

12 crimini **mushrooms, sliced**

2 tablespoons flour

1 cup chicken stock

1 cup heavy cream

1 ten-ounce sack (2 & 1/2 cups), shredded Italian 4-cheese blend **(available on dairy aisle)**

1 can diced tomatoes, **well drained**

1 teaspoon hot sauce **(such as Tabasco) (optional)**

1/2 cup Parmesan **cheese (a couple handfuls)**

Heat a large pot of water to a boil. Salt water and cook pasta to just al dente, about 8 minutes.

In a nonstick skillet, brown and crumble the sausage. Drain cooked crumbles on paper towel-lined plate. Return pan to heat and add evoo, butter, garlic, and mushrooms. Season liberally with salt and pepper. Sauté 3 to 5 minutes, until mushrooms are lightly golden.

Preheat broiler to high.

To mushrooms, add flour and stir, cooking 2 minutes. Whisk in stock, then stir in cream. Bring cream to a bubble, then stir in 2 cups of 4-cheese blend. When cheese has melted into sauce, add tomatoes. When sauce comes to a bubble, remove from heat and adjust seasonings, adding hot sauce, such as Tabasco, if desired.

Combine cheese sauce with sausage and pasta, transfer to a baking dish, casserole, or ovenproof serving platter. Sprinkle remaining 1/2 cup of 4-cheese blend and the grated Parmesan over the top and brown under hot broiler.

miss rachael's MUFFALETTA

1/2 cup giardiniera (pickled vegetables such as cauliflower, carrots, olives, celery, and hot peppers) (found in bulk bins near specialty olives or in jars on Italian foods aisle)

1/2 cup pitted Sicilian green olives or other good-quality large pitted green olives

1 large round loaf crusty bread, 10 to 12 inches

A drizzle of extra-virgin olive oil (evoo)

2 tablespoons chopped fresh rosemary, a couple of sprigs, or 1 teaspoon dried (1/3 palmful)

1/4 pound Genoa salami or sweet sopressata

1/4 pound cappicola spicy ham

1/4 pound sliced provolone cheese

> **TIP**
> Suggested beverages: Italian sodas, mineral water, and beer

Chop giardiniera in a food processor with olives. Split bread, drizzle with evoo, and sprinkle with chopped rosemary. Spread the olive salad on the bottom of the bread very liberally. Pile the meats on top of the olive salad, then layer cheese over meat and cover the giant sandwich with the bread top. Press down to set the sandwich, then cut into 8 pieces.

30 MINUTE MEALS

MENU

Serves 4

PASS ME A HOAGIE

1
•

HERB AND CHEESE OVEN FRIES

2
•

SAUSAGE, PEPPER, AND ONION HOAGIES

3
•

DATE SHAKES

herb and cheese OVEN FRIES

3 all-purpose potatoes, such as russet, cut into thin wedges

2 or 3 tablespoons extra-virgin olive oil (evoo), just enough to coat potatoes

1 teaspoon dried Italian seasoning, or 1/2 teaspoon each dried oregano, thyme, and parsley

Salt and freshly ground black pepper, to taste

1/2 cup grated Parmigiano Reggiano cheese

Preheat oven to 500°F.

Place potato wedges on a cookie sheet. Drizzle with just enough oil to coat. Season with Italian seasoning, salt, and pepper. Roast potatoes and turn after 15 to 20 minutes. Sprinkle cheese liberally on potatoes and roast, another 10 minutes. Serve.

sausage, pepper, and onion HOAGIES

3/4 pound sweet Italian sausage

3/4 pound hot Italian sausage

3 tablespoons extra-virgin olive oil (evoo) (three times around the pan)

2 large cloves garlic, crushed

1 large onion, thinly sliced

2 cubanelle peppers (light-green mild Italian peppers), seeded and thinly sliced

1 red bell pepper, seeded and thinly sliced

Salt and freshly ground black pepper, to taste

2 or 3 hot cherry peppers, banana peppers, or pepperoncini, finely chopped

3 tablespoons hot pepper juice from the jar

Bread

4 crusty, semolina submarine sandwich rolls (8 inches each), sesame seed or plain

1 tablespoon extra-virgin olive oil (evoo)

3 tablespoons butter

1 large clove garlic

1 & 1/2 teaspoons dried Italian seasoning (half palmful), or 1/2 teaspoon each, oregano, thyme, and parsley

Place the sausages in a large nonstick skillet. Pierce the casings with a fork. Add 1 inch water to the pan. Bring liquid to a boil. Cover sausages; reduce heat and simmer, 10 minutes.

Heat a second skillet over medium-high heat. Add 2 tablespoons evoo (twice around the pan). Add garlic, onion, cubanelle, and red peppers. Season with salt and pepper.

Drain sausages and return pan to stove, raising heat back to medium-high. Add the remaining tablespoon evoo (a drizzle) to the skillet; brown and crisp the casings. Remove sausages, slice into 2-inch pieces on an angle and set pieces back in the pan to sear.

Prepare the bread: Preheat the broiler to high.

Split the bread and toast under the broiler. Melt evoo and butter together in a small pan over medium heat. Add garlic and let it sizzle a minute or two. Brush rolls with garlic butter and sprinkle with a little Italian seasoning.

Combine the cooked peppers and onions with the sausages. Add hot peppers and hot pepper juice to the skillet. Toss and turn the sausage, peppers, and onions, picking up all the drippings from the pan. Pile the meat and peppers into the garlic rolls and serve.

date SHAKES

1 cup pitted dates, **coarsely chopped**
1 quart skim milk
2 pints French vanilla ice cream
1 teaspoon grated fresh nutmeg

For each date shake, place 1/4 cup dates (a handful), in a blender. Add 1 cup cold skim milk and 2 big scoops of French vanilla ice cream. Grate 1/4 teaspoon fresh nutmeg into blender and blend until smooth.

SMALL-IDAYS

SMALL HOLIDAY CELEBRATIONS AT HOME

We can't all be The Waltons. I rarely celebrate a holiday by having dinner with 20 relatives, the number they seem to like in Hollywood. Lifestyles have changed, and extended families cannot always get together on holidays. For these reasons, I've written menus for small holiday celebrations, Small-idays, I call them. You will find wonderful recipes for Halloween, Hanukkah, Thanksgiving, Christmas, and New Year's, too. Thanksgiving was a Mt. Everest for a 30-minute cook to conquer. I came, I saw, I climbed, I cooked. And I planted a 30-minute clock at the top!

RACHAEL RAY 30-MINUTE MEALS
gettogethers

30 MINUTE MEALS

MENU

Serves 6

HOWLING GOOD HALLOWEEN

1

CURRIED CARROT SOUP

2

STEAK BITES WITH
BLOODY MARY DIPPING SAUCE

3

ANTI-VAMPIRE GARLIC-LOVERS'
SHRIMP

4

CANDY BOWL

curried CARROT SOUP

Timing note: Start the soup, then the steak and dipping sauce. Prepare garlic for shrimp. Cook steak bites and shrimp at the same time, 5 minutes before you eat.

1 tablespoon extra-virgin olive oil (evoo) (once around the pan)

2 tablespoons butter

1 medium onion, chopped

1 & 1/2 pounds packaged baby carrots (from produce section)

6 cups chicken broth (available on soup aisle)

1 tablespoon mild curry paste or 1 & 1/2 tablespoons curry powder (1 rounded palmful)

1/4 to 1/2 teaspoons ground cayenne pepper

Coarse salt, plus more to taste

1 cup sour cream

Plastic condiment bottle or medium plastic food storage bag

1 toothpick

6 blades fresh chives, cut into 1-inch pieces

Preheat a medium pot over medium-high heat. Add evoo and butter. When butter has melted, add onions and carrots and sauté, 5 minutes. Add 4 cups chicken broth, the curry, cayenne, and salt. Bring to a boil, cover, and cook until carrots are very tender, about 15 minutes. Place pot on a trivet next to a food processor.

Process soup in 2 or 3 small batches until soup is smooth and carrots are fully pureed, transferring processed soup to a large glass bowl as you work. Return completed soup to the soup pot and place back over low heat. If the soup is too thick, add remaining broth, up to 2 cups, to achieve desired consistency. Adjust seasonings.

Place sour cream in a plastic squeeze bottle or into a medium food-storage bag. If using a bag, cut a very small hole in the corner of the bag with scissors. Ladle soup into bowls and squirt a swirl of sour cream around each bowl from the center out to the rim. Drag a toothpick from the center of the bowls out to the edges, forming a spider web design on soup. Pile a few pieces of cut chives at the center of each bowl to resemble green spiders in their webs! Cool!

SMALL HOLIDAY CELEBRATIONS AT HOME

SMALL-IDAYS

STEAK BITES
with bloody mary dipping sauce

1 tablespoon extra-virgin olive oil (evoo) (eyeball it), plus more for drizzling

1 small onion, finely chopped

1/2 cup vodka

2 tablespoons Worcestershire sauce (eyeball it)

2 teaspoons hot sauce (such as Tabasco brand)

1 cup tomato sauce

1 rounded tablespoon prepared horseradish

Salt and freshly ground black pepper, to taste

1 & 1/3 pounds beef sirloin, cut into large bite-size pieces, 1 inch by 2 inches

Steak seasoning blend such as Montreal Seasoning by McCormick or coarse Salt and freshly ground black pepper, to taste

6- to 8-inch bamboo skewers

Make the dipping sauce: Heat a small saucepan over medium heat. Add 1 tablespoon evoo and onions and sauté, 5 minutes. Add vodka and reduce by half. Add Worcestershire, hot sauce, tomato sauce, and horseradish. Stir to combine, and return the sauce to a bubble. Add salt and pepper, and adjust seasonings.

Heat a nonstick skillet over high heat. Coat meat bites lightly in evoo. Season with steak seasoning blend or salt and pepper. Cook meat in hot pan until caramelized all over, about 2 minutes on each side. Transfer dipping sauce to a small dish and place at the center of a serving platter. Surround the dip with steak bites and set several bamboo "stakes" or skewers alongside meat. Makes 6 appetizer servings

anti-vampire garlic-lovers' SHRIMP

12 to 15 cloves garlic, cracked away from skins

2 tablespoons extra-virgin olive oil (evoo) (2 times around the pan)

2 tablespoons butter, cut into small pieces

1/2 to 1 teaspoon crushed red pepper flakes

1 & 1/2 pounds (30 pieces) jumbo shrimp, peeled and deveined (ask for easy-peel shrimp at the seafood counter)

1 teaspoon coarse salt

Freshly ground black pepper, to taste

Process garlic in a food processor to finely chop. Heat a large skillet over medium-high heat. Add evoo and butter. Add garlic and crushed pepper flakes to oil and butter. Season shrimp with salt and toss to coat. Add shrimp to the pan and cook, stirring frequently, until pink and the heads curl to the tails. Add black pepper, to taste. Serve immediately.

CANDY bowl

Glass bowl and clear water glass or tumbler

1 pound black or red licorice twists

2 pounds candy corn

1 pound gummy worms

4 gummy candy rats

Set a water glass in the center of a glass bowl. Fill glass with licorice twists. Fill bowl with candy corn to anchor glass in place. Top candy corn with lots of candy worms. Place the rats around the serving area for your buffet. Add any other favorite candies to this big bowl of fun!

Serves 4

THANKSGIVING-IN-A-FLASH

1

BOURBON-PECAN
SMASHED SWEET POTATOES

2

BRUSSELS SPROUTS WITH
BACON AND SHALLOTS

3

TURKEY CUTLETS WITH
CRANBERRY-ORANGE STUFFING AND
QUICK PAN GRAVY

4

5-MINUTE APPLE CRISP

bourbon-pecan smashed SWEET POTATOES

3 medium sweet potatoes, peeled and cut into chunks

3 tablespoons butter, cut into small pieces

1/2 cup chopped pecans (a couple handfuls)

3 tablespoons brown sugar

2 shots bourbon

1/2 cup orange juice

1/4 to 1/2 teaspoon freshly grated nutmeg

Salt and freshly ground black pepper, to taste

Bring a medium pot of water to a boil. Add sweet potatoes and cook, 12 to 15 minutes, until very tender. Drain sweet potatoes in a colander. Return pan to medium heat. Add butter to the pan. When butter has melted, add pecans and toast, 2 minutes. Add sugar; let it bubble. Add bourbon and cook out alcohol, 1 minute. Add orange juice to the pot and the cooked sweet potatoes. Smash with a masher and season the sweet potatoes with nutmeg, salt, and pepper. Makes 4 BIG servings

BRUSSELS SPROUTS

with bacon and shallots

3 slices bacon, chopped

1 tablespoon extra-virgin olive oil (evoo) (once around the pan)

2 shallots, chopped

1 & 1/2 pounds Brussels sprouts, trimmed, small sprouts left whole, larger sprouts halved

Salt and freshly ground black pepper, to taste

1 cup chicken broth

Brown bacon in a medium skillet over medium-high heat. Drain bacon fat and move bacon to a paper towel-lined plate. Add evoo to the pan, then shallots and sauté, 1 to 2 minutes. Add Brussels sprouts and coat in evoo. Season with salt and pepper. Cook Brussels sprouts, 2 to 3 minutes, to begin to soften, then add broth. Bring broth to a bubble, cover, and reduce heat to medium-low. Cook 10 minutes, until tender. Transfer sprouts with a slotted spoon to a serving dish and top with cooked bacon bits.

SMALL-IDAYS SMALL HOLIDAY CELEBRATIONS AT HOME

TURKEY CUTLETS
with cranberry-orange stuffing and quick pan gravy

Stuffing

    1 tablespoon extra-virgin olive oil (evoo) (once around the pan)
    2 tablespoons butter, cut into small pieces
    2 stalks celery with greens, from the heart of the stalk, chopped
    1 medium onion, chopped
    1 bay leaf, fresh or dried
    Salt and freshly ground black pepper, to taste
    2 cranberry-orange muffins (from the baked goods section)
    A few sprigs fresh thyme, leaves stripped from stems and chopped
        (2 tablespoons)
    1 cup chicken broth

Turkey and Gravy

    1 & 1/3 pounds turkey breast cutlets
    Salt and freshly ground black pepper, to taste
    1 teaspoon poultry seasoning
    2 tablespoons extra-virgin olive oil (evoo)
    2 tablespoons butter, cut into small pieces
    2 tablespoons all-purpose flour
    2 cups chicken broth
    Salt and freshly ground black pepper, to taste
    Chopped fresh flat-leaf parsley, for garnish (optional)

Make the stuffing: To a medium frying pan over moderate heat add evoo and butter. When butter has melted, add celery, onion, and bay. Season with salt and pepper. Split muffins down the center and crumble into pan to combine with vegetables. Add thyme and chicken broth. Cook stuffing 5 minutes, then remove from heat and let stand in warm pan.

Prepare the turkey and gravy: Preheat a large nonstick skillet over medium-high heat. Season turkey cutlets with salt, pepper, and poultry seasoning. Add evoo and sauté 5 minutes on each side, then transfer cutlets to a warm plate and cover plate with aluminum foil. Return skillet to stove and reduce heat a bit. Add butter, then flour to the melted butter. Cook flour and butter a minute or two, stirring with a whisk.

Whisk in chicken broth. Reduce the broth, 2 or 3 minutes, to desired gravy
consistency. Season with salt and pepper, to taste.

To serve, mound stuffing onto dinner plates using an ice cream scoop. Rest sautéed
turkey cutlets on top of the stuffing and cover the turkey with gravy. Garnish with
chopped parsley and serve with sweet potatoes and Brussels sprouts.

5-minute APPLE CRISP

2 cans (15 ounces each) apple pie filling **(found on baking aisle)**
1/2 teaspoon freshly grated nutmeg
1/4 cup firmly packed brown sugar
1 cup granola **or fruit and nut muesli cereal**
1 pint vanilla ice cream

Heat pie filling in a small pot over medium-low heat. Season with nutmeg and spoon into
dessert cups. Top with a sprinkle of brown sugar and a few tablespoons of granola
or muesli. Top with small scoops of vanilla ice cream and serve.

SMALL-IDAYS SMALL HOLIDAY CELEBRATIONS AT HOME

159

30 MINUTE MEALS

MENU

Serves 6

GIVING GRAZIE: ITALIAN-STYLE THANKSGIVING

1
●

TURKEY CUTLETS WITH CORN, SAGE, AND PROSCIUTTO STUFFING

2
●

SAUTÉED PEPPERS WITH PARMESAN CHEESE

3
●

GREEN BEANS WITH STEWED TOMATOES

4
●

BUTTERNUT SQUASH WITH THYME

TURKEY CUTLETS
with corn, sage, and prosciutto stuffing

Turkey

2 pounds turkey breast cutlets **(2 packages) (12 pieces)**

2 teaspoons poultry seasoning

Salt **and freshly ground black** pepper, **to taste**

3 tablespoons extra-virgin olive oil **(evoo)**

2 tablespoons butter

2 tablespoons all-purpose flour

2 cups chicken broth **or canned turkey broth (available around Thanksgiving)**

Stuffing

1 tablespoon extra-virgin olive oil **(evoo)**

2 tablespoons butter

3 stalks celery **from the heart, chopped**

1 medium onion, **chopped**

Salt **and freshly ground black** pepper, **to taste**

2 teaspoons poultry seasoning

4 sprigs fresh sage, **chopped (2 tablespoons)**

2 tablespoons chopped fresh flat-leaf parsley **(eyeball it)**

1/4 pound prosciutto, **deli-sliced like bacon, then chopped**

3 corn muffins, **crumbled**

1 cup chicken broth **or canned turkey broth**

Prepare the turkey and gravy: Heat a large skillet over medium-high heat. Season turkey with poultry seasoning, salt, and pepper. Add 1 & 1/2 tablespoons evoo (1 & 1/2 times around the pan). Brown 6 cutlets, 2 minutes on each side, remove to a plate and repeat with remaining pieces of turkey. Add butter to the pan. When it has melted, whisk in flour and cook a minute. Whisk in broth and bring up to a bubble. Reduce heat to a simmer and slide turkey back into pan to finish cooking in gravy.

Make the stuffing: To a second skillet over medium-high heat, combine evoo and butter. When butter has melted into evoo, add celery and onions and season with salt, pepper, and poultry seasoning. Sauté 5 minutes, until just tender. Add sage, parsley, and prosciutto and stir to combine. Crumble muffins into the pan. Moisten stuffing with broth and heat through. Remove from heat. Cover with foil to keep warm.

When the side dishes are ready, use an ice cream scoop to mound stuffing on plates and top with 2 cutlets each and a small ladleful of gravy.

sautéed PEPPERS with parmesan cheese

2 tablespoons extra-virgin olive oil (evoo) (twice around the pan)
4 cloves garlic, crushed away from skin
2 green bell peppers, seeded and sliced lengthwise into 1/2-inch strips
1 large red bell pepper, seeded and sliced lengthwise into 1/2-inch strips
Salt and freshly ground black pepper, to taste
1/4 cup grated Parmesan cheese (a couple handfuls)
2 tablespoons chopped fresh flat-leaf parsley, for garnish

Heat a skillet over medium-high heat. Add evoo, crushed garlic, and bell peppers. Season with salt and pepper. Sauté until just tender, 6 or 7 minutes. Sprinkle in cheese and remove from heat. Transfer peppers to a platter. Garnish with chopped parsley. Cover with foil to keep warm until ready to serve.

GREEN BEANS with stewed tomatoes

1 large bag (16 ounces) whole frozen green beans
1 can (14 ounces) stewed tomatoes
2 scallions, chopped
Extra-virgin olive oil (evoo), for drizzling (about 2 teaspoons)
Salt and freshly ground black pepper, to taste

In a microwave-safe bowl, combine beans and stewed tomatoes, scallions, and a drizzle of evoo. Loosely cover bowl with plastic wrap and microwave on high, 5 minutes. Stir and microwave on high 2 minutes more. Season with salt and pepper to taste, and serve.

butternut SQUASH with thyme

1/2 cup chicken broth

2 boxes (10 ounces each) frozen cooked butternut squash

2 tablespoons chopped fresh thyme

Salt **and freshly ground black** pepper**, to taste**

1/2 cup grated Parmesan **cheese**

In a medium pot, bring chicken broth to a simmer over medium heat. Add squash and cook together until squash is warm through and loose. Stir in thyme, salt, pepper, and cheese, and cook over low heat to combine flavors. Place in a serving bowl and serve.

TIP

Complete the menu with assorted Italian pastries or pies (store-bought)

Serves 4

THANKSGIVING FOR EVERYDAY

1
●

HERB SMASHED POTATOES
WITH GOAT CHEESE

2
●

TURKEY AND WILD MUSHROOM
MEATLOAF PATTIES
WITH PAN GRAVY

3
●

GREEN BEANS WITH LEMON AND
TOASTED ALMONDS

HERB SMASHED POTATOES
with goat cheese

3 large all-purpose potatoes, peeled and cut into chunks

Salt and freshly ground black pepper, to taste

1 tablespoon extra-virgin olive oil (evoo) (once around the pan)

2 tablespoons butter, cut into pieces

1 shallot, chopped

10 blades chives, chopped or snipped (3 tablespoons)

3 or 4 sprigs fresh thyme, leaves stripped and chopped (2 tablespoons)

1 cup chicken broth

1 small log (4 ounces) herb, peppercorn, or plain goat cheese

Bring a medium pot of water to a boil. Add potatoes and salt. Boil potatoes 15 minutes or until fork-tender.

Begin other dishes for your menu with the pocket of time you have here.

Drain cooked potatoes and return empty pot to stove. Adjust heat to medium. Add evoo, then butter. When butter has melted, add shallots and sauté, 2 to 3 minutes. Add chives and thyme, then potatoes to the pot. Mash potatoes, adding broth as you work to achieve desired consistency. Season with salt and pepper, to taste.

Remove goat cheese from packaging and cut into 4 disks. Serve potatoes on dinner plate and top each mound with a disk of goat cheese.

SMALL-IDAYS SMALL HOLIDAY CELEBRATIONS AT HOME

TURKEY and WILD MUSHROOM MEATLOAF PATTIES with pan gravy

3 tablespoons extra-virgin olive oil (evoo)

8 crimini (baby portobello) mushrooms, chopped

8 shiitake mushrooms, chopped

1 shallot, chopped

Salt and freshly ground black pepper, to taste

1 & 1/3 pounds ground turkey (1 package)

3 or 4 sprigs fresh sage, chopped (about 2 tablespoons)

1 tablespoon Worcestershire sauce (eyeball it)

1/2 cup Italian bread crumbs

1 egg, beaten

2 tablespoons butter

2 tablespoons all-purpose flour

2 cups chicken or turkey broth

1 teaspoon poultry seasoning

Heat a nonstick skillet over medium-high heat. Add 2 tablespoons evoo (twice around the pan). Add chopped mushrooms and shallots and season with salt and pepper. Sauté mushrooms, 5 or 6 minutes, until dark and tender. Remove from heat. Transfer mushrooms to a bowl and return pan to stovetop to preheat to cook patties.

Place turkey in a mixing bowl. Make a well in the center of the meat. Add sage, Worcestershire, bread crumbs, and beaten egg. Scrape sautéed mushrooms and shallots into the bowl. Add salt and pepper. Mix together and make a small, 1-inch patty. Place patty in the hot pan and cook 1 minute on each side. Taste for seasonings and adjust seasonings in meatloaf mixture accordingly. Divide meatloaf mixture into 4 equal parts by scoring the meat before you form patties. Form into oval patties, 1 inch thick. Add 1 tablespoon evoo to the pan, and arrange patties in the pan. Cook 6 minutes on each side and transfer to a serving plate or individual dinner plates. Return pan to heat and add butter. When butter has melted, whisk in flour and cook a minute or two. Whisk in broth and season gravy with poultry seasoning, salt, and pepper, to taste. Thicken gravy to your liking and pour over patties, reserving a little to pass at the table.

GREEN BEANS
with lemon and toasted almonds

1 package (2 ounces) sliced almonds (found on baking aisle)
1 pound green beans, trimmed
1 tablespoon butter
Juice of 1/2 lemon
Salt and freshly ground black pepper, to taste

In a medium pan, toast almonds over medium heat. Remove from pan and add 1/2 inch water to pan. Bring water to a boil, add beans and cover pan. Reduce heat. Cook beans 4 or 5 minutes until just tender yet still green. Drain beans and set aside. Return pan to stovetop and melt butter over moderate heat. Add lemon juice to butter (juice lemon half right-side up to keep seeds in lemon rather than in your beans). Add beans to lemon butter and coat evenly. Season with salt and pepper, to taste. Transfer green beans to dinner plates or serving plate and top with almonds.

TIP
Complete menu with pecan pie and whipped cream (store-bought)

SMALL-IDAYS SMALL HOLIDAY CELEBRATIONS AT HOME

30 MINUTE MEALS

MENU

Serves 6

HAPPY HANUKKAH

1

APRICOT CHICKEN

2

QUICK POTATO AND CARROT
LATKES

3

CHUNKY GOLDEN APPLESAUCE

4

INDIVIDUAL NO-BAKE
STRAWBERRY CHEESECAKES

apricot CHICKEN

2 tablespoons extra-virgin olive oil (evoo) (twice around the pan)

2 pounds chicken tenders, cut in half on an angle

Salt and freshly ground black pepper, to taste

1 large onion, chopped

2 tablespoons cider vinegar or white wine vinegar

12 dried pitted apricots, chopped

2 cups chicken broth

1 cup apricot all-fruit spread or apricot preserves

2 tablespoons chopped or snipped chives, for garnish

Heat a large skillet with a lid over medium-high heat. Add evoo and chicken. Season with salt and pepper. Lightly brown the chicken a few minutes on each side. Add onions and cook, 5 minutes. Add vinegar to the pan and let it evaporate. Add apricots and broth. When broth comes to a bubble, add preserves and stir to combine. Cover pan, reduce heat and simmer, 10 to 15 minutes. Serve chicken with a sprinkle of chopped or snipped chives as garnish.

quick potato and carrot LATKES

Vegetable oil, **for frying**
1 sack (24 ounces) shredded potatoes **for hash browns (available on dairy aisle)**
1 large carrot
1 medium onion
2 eggs, **beaten**
2 teaspoons salt
1 teaspoon baking powder
3 tablespoons matzo meal, **cracker meal, or all-purpose flour**

Heat 1/2 inch oil in a large skillet over medium to medium-high heat. To test oil, add a piece of bread to the pan. It should turn golden brown in a count to 10. Adjust heat as necessary.

Place potatoes in a large bowl. Using a hand grater, grate the carrot and onion into the bowl. Add beaten eggs to the bowl. Add salt and baking powder, then sprinkle in meal or flour. Combine vegetables and meal with a wooden spoon. Drop mixture into oil in 3-inch mounds. Press down gently with spatula to form patties. Fry in batches of 4 to 6 patties (depending on the size of your skillet), 1 inch apart, until golden, about 3 minutes on each side. Drain on paper towel or parchment-lined tray.

chunky golden APPLESAUCE

4 golden delicious apples, **cored and chunked**
2 teaspoons lemon juice
1/2 cup golden raisins
1 cup apple juice **or cider**
3 tablespoons honey **(eyeball it)**

Combine all ingredients in a medium pot and cook over medium to medium-high heat until apples begin to break down and raisins are plump, 10 to 12 minutes. Serve with Quick Potato and Carrot Latkes.

individual no-bake
STRAWBERRY CHEESECAKES

12 strawberries, **hulled**

12 ounces softened cream cheese **(1 & 1/2 eight-ounce bricks)**

2/3 cup sour cream

1 cup confectioners' sugar

1 teaspoon vanilla extract

6 individual graham cracker crusts **(available on baking aisle)**

Coarsely chop 6 berries and place in a food processor. Add cream cheese, sour cream, confectioners' sugar, and vanilla extract and process until smooth. Using a rubber spatula, fill pie shells. Garnish cheesecakes with slices of remaining berries.

30 MINUTE MEALS

MENU

Serves 6

TOP SMALL-IDAY "PICKIES"

1
•

PICKIES:

CRAB DIP WITH ASPARAGUS
AND BAGUETTE

SEARED SCALLOPS WITH BACON AND
SCALLIONS

GRILLED BABY LAMB CHOPS
WITH PARSLEY-MINT PESTO
DIPPING SAUCE

2
•

ALMOND SNOWBALL COOKIES

In my family, we love to graze—have a bite of this, a taste of that. We refer to snack-friendly recipes as "pickies." Here is a tasty menu of some of my favorite holiday pickies.

ALMOND snowball cookies

2 egg whites
A pinch of salt
1/3 cup sugar **(eyeball it)**
1 teaspoon almond extract **(eyeball it)**
1 & 1/2 cups (about 6 ounces) shredded coconut
1/4 teaspoon grated or ground nutmeg
3 tablespoons all-purpose flour
9 candied cherries**, halved**
1/4 cup sliced almonds

Preheat oven to 350°F.

In a mixing bowl, beat egg whites and salt to soft peaks with an electric hand mixer, then add sugar and beat again until peaks are stiff. Beat in almond extract. Using a rubber spatula or wooden spoon, stir in half of the coconut. Sprinkle in the nutmeg and flour, stir, then fold in the last of the coconut.

Using a melon-ball scoop or 2 teaspoons, arrange 9 "snowballs" a couple of inches apart on each of 2 cookie sheets. Bake snowballs 12 to 15 minutes, until lightly golden. Remove from oven and garnish each snowball with a half cherry and a couple of slivered almonds. Transfer to a rack or serving plate to cool. Makes 18 snowballs.

CRAB DIP with asparagus and baguette and seared SCALLOPS with bacon and scallions

1 pound thin asparagus spears, trimmed

4 slices bacon

12 ounces lump crabmeat (found in fresh-packed tubs in seafood department)

2 teaspoons Old Bay Seasoning (a palmful) (found near seafood counter or on spice aisle)

1/2 cup (half an 8-ounce brick) softened cream cheese

1/4 cup sour cream (eyeball it)

8 blades chives, chopped (2 tablespoons)

Juice of 1/2 lemon

1 to 2 teaspoons Tabasco or other brand hot sauce, to taste

Salt and freshly ground black pepper, to taste

18 sea scallops

2 tablespoons extra-virgin olive oil (evoo) or vegetable oil

4 scallions, chopped

1 crusty baguette, sliced at bakery counter

Steam asparagus in 1/2 inch simmering water, covered, for 3 to 5 minutes, until just tender. Cool under running cold water and dry on paper towels.

Crisp bacon in frying pan, under broiler, or in microwave. Work on the dip while bacon cooks. When bacon is crisp, drain and chop. Set aside.

Preheat a nonstick pan over high heat for scallops.

Make the crab dip: Break up crabmeat with your fingertips and check for pieces of shell. Using a rubber spatula or wooden spoon, combine crab with Old Bay, cream cheese, sour cream, chives, lemon juice, and Tabasco. Season dip with salt and pepper, to taste. Transfer to a small bowl to serve.

Season all the scallops with salt and pepper. To very hot skillet, add 1 tablespoon evoo (once around the pan), then place 9 scallops in the pan, an inch apart. Sear scallops 2 minutes on each side, until caramelized and opaque. Transfer to a platter and cover loosely with foil. Repeat with remaining evoo and scallops.

To serve, top scallops with chopped bacon bits and scallions by scattering them evenly over the scallops. Place party picks in a shot glass or small dish and set them on or near platter. Place the crab dip on a large serving platter or board and surround with asparagus spears and sliced baguette for dipping and spreading.

grilled baby LAMB CHOPS
with parsley-mint pesto dipping sauce

1 cup fresh flat-leaf parsley tops (3 handfuls)

1/4 cup (6 to 8 sprigs) fresh mint

1 large clove garlic

1/4 cup (2-ounce package) sliced almonds

1 teaspoon cumin

1/2 teaspoon coriander

Salt and freshly ground black pepper, to taste

1 tablespoon red wine vinegar

1/3 cup extra-virgin olive oil (evoo), plus more for drizzling

2 racks baby lamb, cut into chops by the butcher

Preheat a grill pan or large heavy skillet over medium-high to high heat.

In a food processor, combine parsley, mint, garlic, almonds, cumin, and coriander and pulse-grind until mixture is finely chopped. Add a little salt and pepper and the vinegar to the processor and turn it back on. Stream in evoo until a sauce forms. Stop processor, taste, and adjust seasonings. Transfer to a small bowl using a rubber spatula.

Drizzle chops with evoo, season with salt and pepper, and grill for 3 to 5 minutes on each side for medium-rare to medium-well. Arrange chops around the dipping sauce and serve.

Serves 6

SMALL-IDAY VEGGIE "PICKIES"

1
•

PICKIES:

SPINACH SALAD WITH WARM DIJON DRESSING

ZUCCHINI AU GRATIN

TOMATO-CHEESE-HERB STUFFED MUSHROOMS

SMOKED MOZZARELLA SANDWICHES WITH
PIZZA DIPPING SAUCE

2
•

MAPLE WALNUT ICE CREAM WITH
WARM MAPLE SYRUP
AND SALTED NUTS

Serve these dishes if you would like to please a small group of both meat-eaters and meat-free-ers alike.

ZUCCHINI au gratin

2 tablespoons extra-virgin olive oil (evoo) (twice around the pan)

2 medium zucchinis, thinly sliced on an angle

1 medium onion, sliced

Salt and freshly ground black pepper, to taste

2 tablespoons butter

2 tablespoons all-purpose flour

1 & 1/2 cups milk

1/2 teaspoon grated or ground nutmeg

1/2 cup grated Parmesan cheese

1 cup shredded sharp white cheddar cheese

1 loaf crusty Tuscan or French bread, sliced at bakery counter

Heat a large skillet over medium-high heat. Add 2 tablespoons evoo. Add zucchini and onions, season with salt and pepper and sauté, 10 to 15 minutes, turning frequently, until disks are tender and onions are caramelized at edges.

Preheat broiler to high.

Heat a small saucepan over moderate heat. Add butter and melt. Whisk in flour and cook together a minute or two. Whisk in milk and thicken to gravy-like consistency. Season with salt, pepper, and nutmeg. Stir in grated Parmesan cheese.

Transfer zucchini and onions to a shallow baking dish or casserole. Pour sauce over the veggies and cover with cheddar cheese. Brown cheese under broiler until bubbly. Serve with sliced crusty bread.

tomato-cheese-herb
STUFFED MUSHROOMS

24 crimini mushrooms, cleaned with damp towel

2 tablespoons extra-virgin olive oil (evoo), plus more for drizzling

1 tablespoon butter

1 small onion, chopped (about 1/2 cup)

2 large cloves garlic, chopped

1/2 teaspoon crushed red pepper flakes

SMALL-IDAYS SMALL HOLIDAY CELEBRATIONS AT HOME

1/2 cup white wine (eyeball it)

1 can (14 ounces) diced stewed tomatoes

12 to 15 leaves fresh basil, chopped (1/4 cup)

2 to 3 tablespoons chopped fresh flat-leaf parsley (a handful)

3/4 cup plain bread crumbs

1/2 cup grated Parmesan cheese (a couple handfuls)

Salt and freshly ground black pepper, to taste

Preheat oven to 400°F.

Pop stems out of 18 mushrooms. Arrange the 18 caps on a cookie sheet and drizzle them with a little evoo. Place caps in oven.

To a large hot skillet over medium-high heat, add 2 tablespoons evoo and the butter. When butter has melted into evoo, add onions, garlic, and crushed red pepper to the pan. Chop mushroom stems and the remaining 6 whole mushrooms. Add chopped mushrooms to the onions and garlic. Sauté 5 to 7 minutes, until chopped mushrooms become tender. Add wine and cook it out, 2 minutes. Add tomatoes, basil, and parsley and stir to heat tomatoes and wilt basil. Add bread crumbs and combine to absorb liquid. Stir cheese into stuffing and season with salt and pepper, to taste. Remove mushrooms from the oven and use a melon-ball scoop or 2 teaspoons to fill the caps, mounding the stuffing up as high as you can. Bake 10 minutes to crisp the stuffing, then serve.

SMOKED MOZZARELLA SANDWICHES with pizza dipping sauce

1/3 cup extra-virgin olive oil (evoo) (eyeball it)

1 clove garlic, cracked away from skin

12 slices Italian bread

1 pound smoked mozzarella, sliced

2 roasted red peppers (14 to 16-ounce jar), drained

1 can (14 ounces) pizza sauce

Preheat oven to 400°F.

Heat evoo and garlic in a microwave or in a small pot over medium heat. Brush a cookie sheet with garlic oil. Make 6 smoked mozzarella cheese sandwiches and place on cookie sheet. Brush tops of sandwiches with remaining garlic oil. Bake 10 to 12 minutes, until evenly golden and cheese is melted. Cut into quarters for dipping.

Grind red peppers in a food processor to a smooth puree. Add them to the pan you
used for garlic oil. Combine pizza sauce with peppers and heat through. Transfer to
a serving bowl and surround with cheese sandwiches.

SPINACH SALAD
with warm dijon dressing

1 pound baby spinach **leaves (1 & 1/2 ten-ounce sacks), washed and dried**
1 large shallot, **chopped**
1/2 cup extra-virgin olive oil **(evoo) (eyeball it)**
2 teaspoons Dijon **mustard**
1 tablespoon soy sauce
1 tablespoon red wine vinegar
Salt **and freshly ground black** pepper, **to taste**
Edible flowers, **for garnish (optional)**

Place spinach in a large salad bowl.

Make the dressing: Heat shallots in evoo over medium heat to infuse it with flavor and
warm it. Combine mustard, soy sauce, and vinegar in a small bowl and whisk in the
warm evoo in a slow stream. Pour warm dressing over the spinach and toss to wilt
slightly. Season with salt and pepper and garnish with edible flowers, if desired.

MAPLE WALNUT ICE CREAM
with warm maple syrup and salted nuts

1/2 gallon maple walnut ice cream
1 cup dark amber pure maple syrup
1 & 1/2 cups mixed salted nuts
Store-bought real whipped cream **in a spray can (from dairy aisle)**

Let ice cream sit out 5 or 10 minutes to soften for scooping.

Warm syrup in a microwave or over low heat on stovetop.

Scoop ice cream into large cocktail glasses or dessert bowls. Add nuts to warm syrup.
Top ice cream with spoonfuls of nuts and syrup. Garnish with rosettes of whipped
cream and serve.

SMALL-IDAYS SMALL HOLIDAY CELEBRATIONS AT HOME

179

**30 MINUTE MEALS**

MENU

Serves 6

UK SMALL-IDAY
FIT FOR A QUEEN

1
•

FILLET OF BEEF STEAKS WITH
HORSERADISH SAUCE AND YORKIES
(INDIVIDUAL YORKSHIRE PUDDINGS)

2
•

BUTTERED BEETS

3
•

PEAS WITH ONIONS

4
•

CHERRIES JUBILEE

fillet of BEEF STEAKS with horseradish sauce and yorkies (individual yorkshire puddings)

2 eggs

1 & 1/4 cups sifted cake flour

1 cup beef broth (8 ounces)

1/4 cup water

Pinch of nutmeg

Pinch of salt

1/4 cup vegetable oil or melted butter

6 two-inch beef tenderloin steaks

Salt and freshly ground black pepper, to taste

3 tablespoons butter

2 tablespoons all-purpose flour

1 & 1/2 cups milk

3 rounded tablespoonfuls prepared horseradish

8 blades chives, chopped (2 tablespoons)

1/2 cup Madeira or other dry sherry (optional)

Preheat oven to 375°F.

Make the Yorkies: Beat eggs well with a whisk. Combine eggs with cake flour, then whisk in broth and water. Beat until smooth. Add nutmeg and salt. Whisk again to combine. Grease a 6-cup muffin tin with oil or butter using a pastry brush. Place a teaspoon of batter in each tin and set into oven. Bake 5 minutes, then fill each muffin cavity half full with batter. Bake until golden and popped over, 12 to 15 minutes.

Season meat with salt and pepper. Heat a large nonstick skillet with oven-safe handle over high heat. Sear meat in very hot skillet to caramelize the beef, 3 minutes on each side. Transfer to oven and cook 8 minutes longer for medium-rare meat to 15 minutes for well-done.

TIP
For oven proofing: If you have a rubber-handled pan, wrap the handle twice with aluminum foil for baking.

Meanwhile, make the sauce: In a medium saucepan over medium heat melt 2 tablespoons butter. Combine melted butter with flour and cook a minute longer. Whisk in milk. Cook to thicken milk to gravy consistency, then stir in horseradish, chives, salt, and pepper. Transfer sauce to a serving dish.

Remove meat from oven and transfer to a platter. Return pan to stovetop over moderate heat and deglaze pan with 1/2 cup Madeira or dry sherry, if desired. Add the remaining tablespoon butter to the pan and pour the drippings over steaks. Serve with sauce and hot Yorkshire puddings.

buttered BEETS and PEAS with onions

Two UK-favorite sides in under 10—minutes that is!

4 tablespoons butter
2 tablespoons chopped fresh flat-leaf parsley
2 cans (15 ounces each) sliced beets, drained
Salt, to taste
1 cup frozen pearl onions, defrosted
2 boxes (10 ounces each) frozen baby peas

Make the beets: In a medium skillet over moderate heat melt 2 tablespoons butter, add parsley and sliced beets. Warm through, season with salt and serve.

Make the peas: In a second skillet, also over moderate heat, melt remaining 2 tablespoons butter; add onions and warm through. Add peas and cook 5 minutes. Season with salt and transfer to a serving dish.

TIP

If your stovetop is too crowded when you find your pocket of time to deal with the sides, feel free to use your microwave for either of these dishes, loosely covering beets and peas. Microwave on high, but check them every couple of minutes—you're just warming them through and melting butter.

cherries JUBILEE

2 cans (15 ounces each) whole Bing cherries **in juice, drained and juice**
reserved

1 tablespoon sugar

1 tablespoon cornstarch

1/4 cup Kirsch **or cognac**

2 pints vanilla ice cream

In a small dish, combine a little cherry juice with sugar and starch. In a skillet, heat
remaining juice from cherries over moderate heat. Add sugar and starch mixture.
When juice thickens, add cherries to warm through. Pour in liquor, then flame the
pan to burn off alcohol. Remove cherries from heat. Scoop vanilla ice cream into
large cocktail glasses or dessert dishes and spoon cherries over ice cream.

30 MINUTE MEALS

MENU

Serves 4

FIRST NIGHT FEAST

1

PASTA AL FORNO

2

VEAL INVOLTINI WITH PANCETTA
ON BED OF SPINACH

3

PEARS WITH VANILLA ICE CREAM
AND CHOCOLATE SAUCE

PASTA al forno

Salt and freshly ground black pepper, to taste

1 pound ziti rigate or penne rigate (with lines)

Softened butter, for greasing baking dish

2 tablespoons extra-virgin olive oil (evoo) (twice around the pan)

1 small onion, finely chopped

3 cloves garlic, chopped

1 can (15 ounces) crushed tomatoes

1/2 cup heavy cream

2 pinches cinnamon

3 ounces prosciutto (one thick slice from deli counter), chopped

1/4 to 1/3 cup grated Parmigiano Reggiano cheese

Bring large pot of water to boil, add salt and cook pasta to al dente on the chewy side,
7 minutes. Once pasta water comes to a boil to cook ziti, preheat oven to 500°F.
Butter a medium-size baking dish or casserole. To a medium skillet over medium heat
add evoo. Cook onions and garlic in evoo, 3 to 5 minutes. Stir in tomatoes and
bring to a bubble. Add cream and season sauce with cinnamon, salt, and pepper.
Add chopped prosciutto to sauce and stir with cooked pasta to combine. Adjust
seasonings and transfer pasta to buttered baking dish. Cover pasta with cheese and
place in oven, 10 minutes. Serve hot from oven.

SMALL HOLIDAY CELEBRATIONS AT HOME

SMALL-IDAYS

VEAL INVOLTINI
with pancetta on bed of spinach

1 pound veal scaloppini (from the butcher counter)

1/4 cup chopped fresh flat-leaf parsley (a couple handfuls)

Salt and freshly ground black pepper, to taste

1 pound smoked fresh mozzarella cheese, thinly sliced

1 jar (16 to 18 ounces) roasted red peppers, drained and sliced

1/3 pound pancetta, sliced, or thin-cut bacon (from the deli counter)

2 tablespoons extra-virgin olive oil (evoo) (twice around the pan), plus more for drizzling

1 clove garlic, cracked

1 sack (10 ounces) baby spinach or triple-washed spinach leaves

1/4 to 1/3 cup white wine or dry vermouth

Arrange scaloppini on waxed paper or plastic wrap. Sprinkle with parsley, salt, and pepper. Place a thin layer of cheese and a few slices of roasted pepper on each scaloppini. Roll veal and wrap each roll with a slice of pancetta. Secure with toothpicks.

Fry veal rolls in a thin layer of evoo until golden all over and pancetta is crisp, 5 or 6 minutes. Remove from pan to a warm platter. Return skillet to heat. Add a drizzle evoo and the garlic to pan. Wilt spinach in pan, add a touch of wine or vermouth to lift drippings and combine them with greens. Using tongs, place a bed of spinach on each dinner plate and top with veal rolls. Serve immediately.

pears with VANILLA ICE CREAM
and chocolate sauce

2 cans (15 ounces each) pears **in heavy syrup**
1/4 cup amaretto **or dark rum**
4 ounces bittersweet chocolate chips **or chopped chocolate bar**
1 pint French vanilla ice cream

Drain pears over a small saucepan. Reduce syrup over medium-high heat, 12 to 15 minutes. Stir in liquor and cook 2 minutes longer. Add chocolate and stir to melt. Remove from heat.

Slice pears and place in cocktail glasses. Pour hot chocolate sauce over pears and top glasses with small scoops of vanilla ice cream.

SMALL-IDAYS SMALL HOLIDAY CELEBRATIONS AT HOME

Serves 2

NEW YEAR'S EVE SUPPER

1

HERB CHEESE-TIPPED ENDIVE

2

ARTICHOKE HEARTS WITH LEMON AND PARSLEY

3

SALMON WITH CHAMPAGNE-VANILLA SAUCE WITH RICE WITH ASPARAGUS TIPS

4

RASPBERRY SORBET DESSERTS

herb cheese–tipped ENDIVE, ARTICHOKE HEARTS
with lemon and parsley

1 head endive

3 ounces Boursin **or other soft herb cheese**

2 tablespoons chopped chives

1 can (14 ounces) whole artichoke hearts **in water, drained**

1/2 cup fresh flat-leaf parsley **leaves, coarsely chopped**

Zest of 1 lemon

Juice of 1/2 lemon

1 & 1/2 tablespoons extra-virgin olive oil **(evoo) (eyeball it)**

Salt **and freshly ground black** pepper**, to taste**

Edible flowers**, for garnish (optional)**

Trim endive and separate leaves. Pick out 6 leaves and wrap the leftover endive to add to salad another evening. Spread a rounded teaspoonful of cheese onto the firm end of each leaf. Sprinkle the cheese-tipped ends with chives.

Halve artichoke hearts top to bottom and combine with parsley, lemon zest, and lemon juice. Coat with evoo, toss, and season with salt and pepper. Divide the artichokes between 2 plates and garnish each plate with 3 cheese-filled pieces of endive and a few edible flowers.

RICE with ASPARAGUS TIPS

1 tablespoon extra-virgin olive oil **(evoo)**

1 shallot**, chopped**

1 can (14 ounces) chicken broth

1 cup long-grain white rice

1 bundle (3/4 pound) thin asparagus **spears**

Preheat a medium saucepan over medium heat. Add evoo and shallot. Sauté shallot, 1 or 2 minutes. Add broth and bring to a boil. Add rice and stir. When broth returns to a boil, cover and reduce heat to simmer. Cook 18 minutes, until rice is tender.

Trim asparagus of tough bottoms and cut tops into 1-inch pieces on an angle. Steam in 1 inch of water, 3 minutes; drain. Remove rice from heat, fluff with fork, combine with asparagus, and serve.

SMALL-IDAYS   SMALL HOLIDAY CELEBRATIONS AT HOME

SALMON with champagne-vanilla sauce

2 six-ounce salmon **fillets**
Salt **and freshly ground black** pepper, **to taste**
2 tablespoons extra-virgin olive oil **(evoo)**
1 large or 2 small shallots, **finely chopped**
1 split dry champagne
1 whole vanilla bean
1/2 cup heavy cream
2 tablespoons chopped fresh flat-leaf parsley

Heat a nonstick skillet over medium-high heat. Season fish with salt and pepper. Add 1 tablespoon evoo to the pan, then add fish. Cook salmon, 3 minutes on each side, 5 minutes if you like your fish well done. Transfer fish to a serving plate or dinner plates and cover with foil to keep warm.

Add remaining tablespoon of evoo to the pan, pouring once around the pan in a slow stream. Add shallots and cook, 2 minutes. Add champagne to the pan and cook to reduce by half. Split the vanilla bean in half lengthwise and scrape the seeds into champagne. Add cream to the pan and reduce heat to low. Simmer 5 minutes. Pour sauce over fish and serve.

raspberry SORBET desserts

1 pint raspberry sorbet
1/2 pint fresh raspberries
2 ounces Chambord **raspberry liqueur (optional)**
4 sprigs fresh mint, **2 sprigs chopped, 2 left whole**
Piroline **or other rolled dessert cookies**

Scoop sorbet into large cocktail glasses or dessert cups. Top with fresh raspberries, Chambord (if desired), and chopped mint. Garnish with sprigs of mint and rolled cookies.

Serves 4

NEW YEAR'S DAY FEAST

1
•

PÂTÉ AND TOAST WITH ACCESSORIES

2
•

ROASTED BUTTERFLIED
CORNISH HENS

3
•

WHITE AND WILD RICE WITH CHIVES
AND BROCCOLI FLORETS WITH
RED BELL PEPPERS

4
•

NUTKINS:
FROZEN DRINKS WITH ICE CREAM AND
NUT-FLAVORED LIQUEURS

PÂTÉ and toast with accessories

4 slices whole-grain or dark bread, toasted
1/2 pound mousse pâté, any variety
1 large shallot, very thinly sliced
3 tablespoons capers
1 jar (12 ounces) cornichons or baby gherkin pickles

Spread each slice of toast liberally with mousse pâté. Cut each toast diagonally into 4 triangles. Top each triangle with sliced shallots and capers. Arrange toasts on a serving plate or individual plates and garnish with cornichons or baby gherkins.

roasted butterflied CORNISH HENS

4 Cornish hens, butterflied
Salt and freshly ground black pepper, to taste
4 or 5 sprigs fresh rosemary, leaves stripped and
    chopped (3 tablespoons)

3 tablespoons fresh thyme, chopped
3 tablespoons extra-virgin olive oil (evoo)

TIP

To butterfly the Cornish hens, cut along the backbone from the neck to the tail and whack them flat with a heavy frying pan, then cut off the wing tips with kitchen shears. A good butcher will do this for you.

Evenly space 2 racks in oven and preheat to 500°F. Place birds in a large bowl and coat with salt, pepper, herbs, and evoo. Arrange the birds on 2 shallow baking trays, breast side down. Roast birds 10 minutes. Reduce heat to 400°F, flip the birds and roast 15 minutes longer. Remove from oven, fold birds over and serve 1 per person.

white and wild RICE with chives

2 cups chicken broth
3 tablespoons wild rice
1 cup enriched white rice
2 tablespoons butter
3 tablespoons chopped chives

Bring broth to a boil. Add wild and white rice and butter. Return broth to a boil and cover, reduce heat to medium-low. Simmer rice 20 minutes, until tender. Add chives and fluff rice with a fork, then serve.

BROCCOLI florets with red bell peppers

1 pound broccoli florets (available in ready-to-cook bags in produce department)
2 tablespoons extra-virgin olive oil (evoo) (twice around the pan)
1 red bell pepper, seeded, quartered lengthwise, then thinly sliced
Salt and freshly ground black pepper, to taste

Simmer broccoli florets in 1 inch boiling water for 3 minutes, covered. Drain and remove broccoli from the skillet. Return pan to the stovetop over medium heat. Add evoo to the pan and sauté sliced red bell peppers, 2 or 3 minutes. Add the broccoli back to the pan and toss to combine with peppers. Season with salt and pepper to taste, then remove from heat and serve.

NUTKINS: frozen drinks with ice cream and nut-flavored liqueurs

2 ounces Frangelico hazelnut liqueur
2 pints vanilla ice cream
6 ounces Amaretto di Sarrano (4 shots)
1 pint half-and-half
8 ice cubes
Nutmeg, freshly grated or ground, for garnish

In a blender combine 1 ounce Frangelico (just over half a shot), 4 scoops vanilla ice cream, 3 ounces (2 shots) Amaretto, 1 cup half-and-half, and 4 ice cubes. Blend until smooth. Pour into 2 large cocktail glasses, garnish with a sprinkle of freshly grated or ground nutmeg, and repeat with remaining ingredients.

Serves 4

MAKE A HOLIDAY OF ANY DAY

1
•

RACK OF LAMB WITH CRANBERRY-POMEGRANATE SAUCE

2
•

CREAMY POLENTA WITH SAGE AND PANCETTA

3
•

BRAISED RED SWISS CHARD

4
•

MOLASSES COOKIE ICE CREAM SANDWICHES

rack of LAMB with cranberry-pomegranate sauce,
braised red SWISS CHARD,
creamy POLENTA with sage and pancetta

Lamb

2 racks of lamb (ask the butcher to trim and French)
(about 2 & 3/4 pounds total)

Extra-virgin olive oil (evoo), for drizzling

Salt and freshly ground black pepper, to taste

1 cup cranberry juice concentrate

1 pomegranate, seeds picked from shell

1 cup chicken broth

1/2 cup dried sweetened cranberries (a couple handfuls), such as
Crasins, Ocean Spray brand

Swiss Chard

1 tablespoon extra-virgin olive oil (evoo) (once around the pan)

1 small onion, chopped

5 cups clean, coarsely chopped red Swiss chard (1 large bunch)

1 cup vegetable stock

2 handfuls golden raisins

Salt and freshly ground black pepper, to taste

1/2 teaspoon freshly grated nutmeg (eyeball it)

Polenta

1 tablespoon extra-virgin olive oil (evoo)

4 slices pancetta, chopped (available at deli counter)

3 cups chicken broth

1 cup quick-cooking polenta (available on Italian foods or specialty
aisles)

3 sprigs fresh sage, leaves stripped and chopped (2 tablespoons)

2 tablespoons butter, cut into small pieces

Salt and freshly ground black pepper, to taste

10 blades fresh chives, snipped or finely chopped, for garnish

Preheat a grill pan to high and oven to 400°F.

Prepare the lamb: Drizzle lamb with evoo and season with salt and pepper. Grill over
high heat for 2 or 3 minutes on each side. Transfer to a baking sheet or broiler pan

and place in hot oven. Cook 12 to 15 minutes, to 130°F on meat thermometer for rare, 155°F for well. Let meat rest 5 to 10 minutes before serving for juices to redistribute.

Prepare the chard: Heat a large skillet over medium-high heat. Add evoo and onion. Sauté onion 2 minutes, then add chard in bunches until the greens wilt down enough to fit in pan. Add vegetable stock and raisins. Season greens with salt, pepper, and freshly grated nutmeg. Reduce heat to medium-low and cook 10 to 15 minutes, until greens are tender and no longer bitter.

Start the sauce for the lamb: Place cranberry juice concentrate and seeds from pomegranate in a small saucepan and simmer together over low heat, 10 minutes. Strain and return to pan. Meanwhile, combine broth and dried, sweetened cranberries in a bowl. Cover and microwave on high for 1 minute. Let stand 10 minutes to reconstitute cranberries.

Make the polenta: Heat a medium saucepan over medium-high heat. Add evoo and pancetta. Brown pancetta a minute or two and remove from pan to a paper towel-lined plate. Return pan to heat and add chicken broth; bring to a boil. Stir in polenta and stir constantly until mixture masses, 2 or 3 minutes. Remove polenta from heat and stir in sage, butter, pancetta bits, salt, and pepper to taste. Reserve the chives for garnish.

Add cranberries and stock to the strained pomegranate syrup. Heat through to a bubble and remove from stove.

To serve, allow 1/2 rack of lamb per person. Separate chops by singles or by twos and glaze with cranberry-pomegranate sauce. Serve with sage and pancetta polenta garnished with chives and braised red chard.

molasses cookie
ICE CREAM SANDWICHES

8 soft molasses cookies, **such as Archway Homestyle, 3 inches in diameter**

1 pint vanilla ice cream

Line up 4 molasses cookies, bottoms up. Top each with one a well-rounded scoop of vanilla ice cream. Top each ice cream ball with another cookie, forming a sandwich and push down lightly to flatten the ice cream out towards the edges. Serve or wrap and freeze for later.

DINNER AT EIGHT

BETTER THAN A RESTAURANT 24/7

There's something so romantic about the phrase, "Dinner at Eight." I see a restaurant filled with candle-lit tables draped in white tablecloths, waiters in black tie balancing trays of perfect Martinis. On the dance floor, in front of the 13-piece orchestra, pretty ladies in small, black dresses dance cheek to cheek with handsome men in dark suits. SIGH. All of that glamour might be a bit much to produce in 30 minutes. However, if you want to invite several couples over to enjoy cocktails, conversation, and tasty food, these menus will make you look *absolutely fabulous, D-ahh-rling*! Cheek to cheek dancing is allowed, as long as you move the coffee table first!

RACHAEL RAY 30-MINUTE MEALS
gettogethers

30 MINUTE MEALS

MENU

Serves 10

COOKING FOR 10
IN 30

1

SELECT SOFT CHEESE BOARD

2

BALSAMIC
PORK TENDERLOINS

3

ROASTED RATATOUILLE
VEGETABLES

4

TORTELLINI WITH
SPINACH-WALNUT PESTO

select SOFT CHEESE board

2 tins (10 ounces each) smoked almonds

1/2 pound wedge brie with herbs

1/2 pound wedge Saga blue cheese

1 log (6 ounces) goat cheese, any variety

1 baguette, sliced at bakery counter

1 package Carr's assorted crackers or other brand of cracker assortment

1 pound grapes, black, red, or green, separated into small bunches

Pour nuts into a large brandy snifter and set on cheese board. Arrange cheeses with baguette slices and crackers. Decorate with clusters of grapes. Place a few spreaders near cheeses and set out where guests will gather.

balsamic PORK TENDERLOINS

4 & 1/2 pounds pork tenderloin (2 packages with 2 tenderloins per package)

Balsamic vinegar, for drizzling (about 3 tablespoons)

Extra-virgin olive oil (evoo), for drizzling

8 cloves garlic, cracked

Steak seasoning blend such as Montreal Seasoning by McCormick or coarse salt and freshly ground black pepper

4 sprigs each fresh rosemary and thyme, leaves stripped and finely chopped

Preheat oven to 500°F.

Trim silver skin or connective tissue off tenderloins with a thin, very sharp knife. Place tenderloins on a nonstick cookie sheet with a rim. Coat tenderloins in a few tablespoons of balsamic vinegar, rubbing vinegar into meat. Drizzle tenderloins with evoo, just enough to coat. Cut small slits into meat and disperse chunks of cracked garlic cloves into meat. Combine steak seasoning blend or coarse salt and pepper with rosemary and thyme and rub meat with blend. Roast in hot oven 20 to 25 minutes. Let meat rest, transfer to a carving board, slice and serve.

DINNER AT 8 BETTER THAN A RESTAURANT 24/7

199

roasted RATATOUILLE vegetables

1 large red bell pepper, seeded and cut lengthwise into 1-inch strips
1 medium onion, sliced
1 medium eggplant sliced into 1/2-inch pieces slices piled and quartered
1 zucchini, sliced 1/2-inch thick
4 plum tomatoes, seeded and quartered lengthwise
6 cloves garlic, crushed
Extra-virgin olive oil (evoo), to coat
4 sprigs fresh rosemary, chopped (3 tablespoons)
Coarse salt and freshly ground black pepper, to taste

Preheat oven to 500°F.

Working on a cookie sheet, combine vegetables and garlic. Drizzle liberally with evoo and season with rosemary, salt, and pepper. Toss to coat vegetables evenly. Roast until just tender, 15 minutes. Transfer to a serving platter.

TORTELLINI with spinach-walnut pesto

2 pouches (2 ounces each) chopped walnuts (from baking aisle)
Salt and freshly ground black pepper, to taste
2 family-size packages (18 ounces each) cheese- or mushroom-and-cheese-filled fresh tortellini (sold on dairy aisle)
1 cup chicken broth
1 package (10 ounces) baby spinach, a few leaves reserved for garnish
2 cloves garlic
2/3 cup grated Parmigiano Reggiano or Romano cheese
1/4 teaspoon ground or freshly grated nutmeg
1/4 cup extra-virgin olive oil (evoo) (eyeball it)
Edible flowers, for garnish (optional)

Toast walnut pieces in a small pan or toaster oven until lightly browned. Remove to cool.

Place a large pot of water on to boil. Salt water and cook tortellini to package directions.

Heat 1 cup chicken broth to a boil and remove from heat.

Working in batches with a food processor, grind spinach with nuts, chicken broth, and garlic. Transfer to a large bowl. Stir in cheese, nutmeg, evoo, salt, and pepper to taste. Toss hot, cooked tortellini with sauce, then turn pasta out onto a serving platter and garnish with a few baby spinach leaves and edible flowers, if desired.

30 MINUTE MEALS

MENU

Serves 6

SANTA FE
MEAT-FREE FEAST

1

CALABACITAS CASSEROLE WITH
POLENTA AND CHEESE

2

GRILLED GREEN CHILE
QUESADILLAS

3

MEXICAN ICE CREAM PIE

This is another great menu to entertain with that was designed to please both meat eaters and meat-free-ers alike. I am not a veg-head, but I eat meat-free meals often, and some of my friends and co-workers are vegetarians or they are partnered with vegetarians. More and more, I find a need to cook recipes that can please both groups of eaters at the same time. This menu has some real all-veggie favorites inspired by a recent trip to Santa Fe. Enjoy!

mexican ice cream PIE

1 jar (8 ounces) chocolate fudge topping

1 graham cracker piecrust (available on baking aisle)

3 pints coffee or vanilla ice cream, softened in microwave on defrost 30 seconds

2 cups small breakfast cereal flakes, such as Grape Nuts Flakes or Special K

1 teaspoon ground cinnamon

1 tablespoon cocoa powder or instant hot cocoa beverage mix

1/4 cup (2 ounces) Spanish peanuts

Honey, for drizzling

1 canister real whipped cream (from dairy aisle) (optional)

Take the lid off fudge sauce and heat 10 seconds in a microwave on high to make it spreadable. Cover bottom of graham cracker crust with a thin layer of fudge sauce. Fill and mound the crust with coffee or vanilla ice cream using a rubber spatula. Smooth the top of the pie with a spatula, making the surface of the pie smooth and free of lumps. Mix cereal, cinnamon, cocoa, and nuts. Using handfuls of the mix, coat the pie liberally with topping, pressing it into the ice cream as you apply it. Cover pie with plastic storage wrap and set in freezer to set.

When ready to serve, cut pie into 6 wedges. Drizzle each slice with honey and garnish with rosette of whipped cream.

calabacitas CASSEROLE
with polenta and cheese

2 tubes (16 ounces each) prepared polenta

3 tablespoons extra-virgin olive oil (evoo)

2 cups frozen corn kernels, defrosted

4 cloves garlic, chopped

1 green chile pepper, seeded and chopped, or 2 jalapeños, seeded and chopped

2 small to medium zucchini, diced

1 small to medium yellow squash, diced

1 large yellow onion, chopped

Salt and freshly ground black pepper, to taste

2 teaspoons dark chili powder

1 can (14 ounces) stewed tomatoes

2 cups (10 ounces) shredded Monterey Jack cheese (available preshredded on the dairy aisle)

3 scallions, chopped

2 tablespoons chopped cilantro or fresh flat-leaf parsley

Preheat oven to 500°F.

Cut one tube of polenta into 1/2-inch slices lengthwise. Drizzle 1 tablespoon evoo (just eyeball it) into a shallow baking dish or casserole. Spread the oil around with a pastry brush to evenly coat the bottom and sides of the dish. Line the bottom of the dish with the long slices of polenta. Slice the remaining tube of polenta in 1/2-inch slices across, making several disks of polenta. Reserve.

Heat a large skillet over medium-high heat. Add remaining 2 tablespoons evoo, the corn, garlic, and chiles. Sauté 3 minutes, add zucchini, yellow squash, and onions; season with salt, pepper, and chili powder; cook 7 to 8 minutes. Add stewed tomatoes and heat through. Transfer vegetables to baking dish. Top with reserved polenta and the cheese. Place in hot oven to melt cheese and warm polenta, 8 to 10 minutes. Garnish with chopped scallions and cilantro or parsley.

grilled green chile QUESADILLAS

3 fresh chile peppers, such as poblanos, any variety may be used, according to your tolerance for heat

4 large (12-inch) flour tortillas

1 & 3/4-pound brick smoked cheddar, shredded (3 cups)

1 cup salsa verde (available on chip and snack aisle or in Mexican foods section)

1 cup sour cream

2 tablespoons chopped fresh cilantro, for garnish

Heat a grill pan over high heat. Place whole chiles on grill and char all over, 10 minutes. Remove from heat and split chiles. Scrape away seeds with a spoon and slice.

Heat a large nonstick skillet or griddle over medium-high heat. Char the tortilla and blister it on one side, 20 seconds, then flip tortilla. Cover half of the tortilla with cheese and chiles, then fold over. Press down gently with spatula. Cook quesadilla 15 seconds more on each side, transfer to a cutting board. Repeat. Pile up 2 completed quesadillas at a time and cut into 3 generous wedges. The yield will be 12 pieces from 4 quesadillas.

Serve slices on a large platter with small dishes of salsa verde and sour cream for topping. Garnish the platter and toppings with chopped cilantro.

30
MINUTE
MEALS

MENU

Serves 6

JAPANESE-STYLE BARBECUE PARTY

1
●

CHICKEN YAKITORI

2
●

BEEF STRIPS
WITH GINGER AND SOY

3
●

SPICY AHI BITES

CHICKEN yakitori,
BEEF STRIPS with ginger and soy,
SPICY AHI bites

2 & 3/4 cups water

1 & 1/2 cups short-grain white rice

Chicken

3 tablespoons dry sherry

2 tablespoons sugar

1/4 cup tamari (dark soy sauce)

2 tablespoons light-colored oil, such as wok oil or vegetable oil (eyeball it)

1 pound chicken breast tenders, cut in half on an angle

5 scallions, cut in half

Beef

3 inches fresh gingerroot, minced or grated with hand grater or microplane

1/4 cup tamari (dark soy sauce)

2 tablespoons light-colored oil, such as wok oil or vegetable oil (eyeball it)

1 teaspoon toasted sesame oil

1 & 1/4 pounds beef sirloin, 1 & 1/2-inch thick

Steak seasoning blend such as Montreal by McCormick, or salt and freshly ground black pepper, to taste

1 package, minimum 40 count, 8-inch bamboo skewers

Ahi

3 tablespoons sesame seeds (2 palmfuls)

1 tablespoon Chinese 5-spice powder

2 tablespoons steak seasoning blend, such as Montreal Steak Seasoning by McCormick, or salt and freshly ground black pepper, to taste

2 ahi tuna steaks (8 ounces each), cut into 1-by-3-inch pieces

Light-colored oil, such as wok oil or vegetable oil, for drizzling

1 teaspoon toasted sesame oil

Condiments

1 jar (14 to 18 ounces) pickled watermelon rind

1 small jar (10 to 12 ounces) pickled ginger

1 jar (14 to 18 ounces) pickled onions

Fresh Fruit

3 kiwis

3 tangerines

3 Asian pears

Place water in a medium saucepan over high heat and bring to a boil. Add rice, stir. Cover and reduce heat to low. Cook rice 18 minutes or until tender.

Preheat coals for a tabletop hibachi or preheat a grill pan over medium-high to high heat.

Prepare the chicken: Combine sherry, sugar, tamari, and oil in a shallow dish. Turn chicken and scallions in marinade and let stand 10 minutes. Wash your hands.

Prepare the beef: Combine ginger, soy, vegetable oil, and sesame oil in a second shallow dish. Cut raw beef against the grain into thin strips. Thread strips onto skewers, reserving several skewers for chicken. Set beef skewers into ginger-and-soy mixture. Season meat lightly with steak seasoning blend and turn in ginger and soy to coat. Set aside. Wash your hands.

Prepare the tuna: Toast sesame seeds in a small skillet over moderate heat until they pop and are lightly toasted. This process will develop the flavor of the sesame. Combine sesame seeds with 5-spice powder and grill seasoning blend on a piece of waxed paper or on a plate. Coat tuna with a drizzle of light oil to help seeds and spices adhere to fish. Coat fish pieces in sesame and spice mixture.

Cook chicken pieces and scallions in a single layer over hot coals or on hot grill pan for 3 or 4 minutes on each side. Transfer chicken and scallions to a serving plate and set several bamboo skewers on the edge of the plate for spearing meat and scallions.

Place beef skewers on hot grill surface and cook 2 to 3 minutes on each side in a single layer, turning once. Transfer to a serving plate.

Cook fish on hot grill surface, 2 minutes on each side, and transfer to a serving plate. Tuna will be rare. Cook longer, if desired. Drizzle with sesame oil as a condiment. Serve with several bamboo skewers piled on the edge of the plate for spearing the fish.

Transfer pickled watermelon rind, pickled ginger, and pickled onions to ramekins and place alongside grilled meats and fish as condiments. Serve with hot rice and extra soy sauce. Kiwis, tangerines, and Asian pears are a nice offering of fresh fruit to round out this light menu.

30
MINUTE
MEALS

MENU

Serves 6

THAI IT
THEY'LL LIKE IT
DINNER

1
●

THAI CUCUMBER AND RADISH SALAD

2
●

COCONUT SHRIMP

3
●

CHICKEN SATAY STIR-FRY WITH
ORANGE-SCENTED JASMINE RICE

4
●

GINGER SNAP ICE CREAM
SANDWICHES

TIMING NOTE: To serve all of the courses at once—a mix-'n-match, family-style presentation—you can bread the shrimp and wait to heat the oil and fry when you are ready to put the chicken stir-fry in the pan. Or for separate courses, serve the shrimp with the salad, have your rice cooking and your ingredients prepped for the stir-fry, then stir-fry the chicken only when guests are ready for it.

thai cucumber and radish SALAD

1/2 cup rice wine vinegar

3 tablespoons sugar

2 tablespoons light-colored oil, such as canola or safflower

1 pound daikon radish, peeled and thinly sliced

1 English (seedless) cucumber, thinly sliced

1 red bell pepper, seeded and very thinly sliced

1 teaspoon crushed red pepper flakes

20 leaves fresh basil

In the bottom of a medium bowl, combine vinegar, sugar, and oil. Add daikon, cucumber, bell pepper, and pepper flakes. Toss and combine. Cover and chill until ready to serve.

When ready to serve, tear basil into pieces and add to salad. Toss salad to incorporate basil and serve.

coconut SHRIMP

Canola or safflower oil, for frying

1/2 cup plain bread crumbs (a couple handfuls)

2 pinches ground cayenne pepper

1 1/2 teaspoons Chinese 5-spice powder (available on spice aisle)

1 lime

1 cup shredded unsweetened coconut

2 egg whites

1 pound large fantail shrimp, deveined and peeled (ask for easy-peels at seafood counter of market)

1/2 teaspoon salt (eyeball it)

Heat 2 inches oil in a large skillet over medium-high heat. A cube of bread should brown in a count to 10 when oil is ready.

Season bread crumbs with cayenne pepper and 5-spice powder. Grate the zest of the lime and add it to the bread crumbs. Wedge the lime and reserve.

Toss coconut with seasoned bread crumbs to combine. Lightly beat the egg whites. Dip shrimp in the egg whites, then coat with the coconut breading. Fry shrimp 5 minutes in hot oil until evenly golden and crispy. Salt lightly, garnish with lime wedges and serve.

chicken satay STIR-FRY
with orange-scented jasmine rice

Rice

3 & 3/4 cups water

Grated zest of 2 oranges

2 cups jasmine rice, rinsed

Stir-Fry

2 tablespoons canola or safflower oil (twice around the pan)

1 & 1/2 to 1 & 3/4 pounds chicken breast tenders (2 packages), sliced on an angle into bite-size pieces

3 cloves garlic, crushed

1 medium yellow onion, sliced

1 red bell pepper, seeded, quartered, and sliced

1 cup shredded carrots (available preshredded on produce aisle), or 2 medium carrots cut into matchsticks

6 scallions, cut on an angle into 2-inch pieces

1 cup snow peas (a couple handfuls)

Satay Sauce

1/4 cup chunky peanut butter

3 tablespoons tamari (dark soy sauce)

3 tablespoons honey

1 inch gingerroot, peeled and minced

1 clove garlic, crushed

1 teaspoon crushed red pepper flakes

Juice of 1/2 orange

Garnish

- 1/4 cup (2 ounces) chopped peanuts or nut topping (available on the baking aisle)
- 2 to 3 tablespoons chopped cilantro or fresh flat-leaf parsley, for garnish

Make the rice: Heat water with orange zest to boiling. Add rice, return to boil, stir. Cover pot and reduce heat to simmer. Cook rice until tender, 18 minutes. Fluff with fork.

Make the stir-fry: Heat a large nonstick skillet over high heat. Add chicken, garlic, and onion; stir-fry 3 minutes. Add remaining veggies and stir-fry 5 minutes more.

Make the sauce: Heat all sauce ingredients together in a small pot over low heat, stirring until all ingredients are combined.

Transfer stir-fry to a large platter and pour sauce evenly over the chicken and vegetables. Sprinkle the platter with chopped nuts and cilantro. Serve jasmine rice in a separate dish with an ice cream scoop—it makes perfect, pretty, round portions of rice on the dinner plates.

GINGER SNAP ice cream sandwiches

- 2 pints ice cream, coconut, vanilla, or rum raisin
- 24 ginger snap cookies

Soften ice cream in microwave, 10 seconds on high for each pint. Scoop ice cream onto a ginger snap, top with another snap and press to set sandwich. Place sandwiches on a platter and serve or individually wrap and store in freezer.

30 MINUTE MEALS

MENU

Serves 6

MEDITERRANEAN MEAT-FREE DINNER

1

GARLIC AND RED PEPPER
PITA CHIPS WITH
GREEN OLIVE HUMMUS

2

VEGETABLE AND
COUSCOUS STACKS

3

BLACKBERRY NAPOLEONS

blackberry NAPOLEONS

2 half-pint containers blackberries

2 tablespoons granulated sugar

18 wonton wrappers

3 tablespoons butter, **melted**

1/4 cup light-brown sugar

Store-bought real whipped cream **in a spray can (from dairy aisle of market)**

Preheat oven to 400°F.

Combine berries with granulated sugar and let stand 20 minutes.

Meanwhile, arrange wontons on a nonstick cookie sheet. Brush with melted butter and sprinkle with brown sugar. Bake 5 to 7 minutes, until deep golden. Remove from oven and cool until ready to serve.

To assemble, layer 3 pieces of toasted wonton with whipped cream and berries. Repeat to assemble 6 individual Napoleons.

vegetable and couscous STACKS

2 cloves garlic, **cracked away from skin**

1 cup extra-virgin olive oil **(evoo)**

1 medium eggplant, **sliced 1/2 inch thick**

1 medium zucchini, **thinly sliced on an angle**

4 or 5 sprigs rosemary, **leaves stripped and finely chopped (3 tablespoons)**

7 or 8 sprigs fresh thyme **leaves, leaves stripped and chopped (3 tablespoons)**

Coarse salt **and freshly ground black** pepper, **to taste**

2 roasted red peppers **(available in bulk near deli or in jars), drained and quartered**

6 thin (1/2-inch) slices red onion

1 can chicken broth **(about 2 cups), empty can reserved**

2 cups couscous

1/2 cup grated Parmesan **cheese**

1 pound fresh smoked mozzarella, **sliced into 12 thin slices**

12 leaves fresh basil

2 vine-ripe tomatoes, **thinly sliced**

Preheat oven to 400°F. Preheat a grill pan to high.

Warm garlic and evoo on stovetop over low heat. Brush eggplant and zucchini slices lightly with garlic oil and arrange in single layers on 2 cookie sheets. Season with about 2 tablespoons each of rosemary and thyme. Add salt and pepper to the vegetables and place in oven to roast until tender, 15 minutes.

Brush peppers and onions with garlic oil and grill until charred and just tender. Season with salt and pepper.

Pour broth into a saucepan and bring to a boil with 2 tablespoons of the remaining garlic oil. Take the top and bottom off the broth can with a can opener. Rinse can and reserve. When stock boils, remove from heat. Add remaining 1 tablespoon each rosemary and thyme and the couscous. Cover and let stand 5 minutes. Fluff the couscous with a fork and toss with grated cheese.

To assemble, place the can upright on a large serving platter. Set 2 slices of eggplant down into can, then 2 slices zucchini. Press the vegetables down as you work using a rubber spatula to help you. Pack a rounded 1/2 cup couscous into the can, then a piece of grilled roasted red pepper and a thin slice of onion. Next, 2 thin slices smoked mozzarella, 2 leaves basil, and finally, 2 thin slices tomato. Season top of the stack with salt and pepper and garnish with any remaining basil or mixed sprigs of herbs. Remove can and repeat 5 more times with remaining ingredients.

garlic and red pepper PITA CHIPS
with green olive hummus

3 pita breads, 6 to 8 inches in diameter

2 cloves garlic, minced

1/4 cup extra-virgin olive oil (evoo)

2 teaspoons crushed red pepper flakes

Salt, to taste

1 & 1/2 cups store-bought roasted garlic hummus any brand

10 to 12 large green pitted olives, chopped (1/2 cup) (available near deli in bulk bins), plain, herb, or hot pepper flavored

2 scallions, thinly sliced

Preheat oven to 400°F.

Separate each pita, making 6 pieces out of 3 pitas. Stack breads and cut into 6 wedges, making 36 pieces total. Combine garlic, evoo, and 1 teaspoon red pepper flakes in the bottom of a bowl. If you have garlic oil remaining from the previous recipe for vegetable stacks, that may be used up in this recipe, just add crushed red pepper flakes and no garlic. Add pita bread wedges and toss with your fingertips to combine and coat evenly. Scatter the wedges in a single layer on a cookie sheet and bake 5 minutes until browned and crisp. Season hot pita chips with a sprinkle of coarse salt.

Combine hummus with the remaining 1 teaspoon crushed red pepper flakes and chopped green olives. Transfer to a bowl and garnish with scallions. Surround with pita chips and serve.

30
MINUTE
MEALS

MENU

Serves 4

NIGHT-LIGHT

1

BABY SPINACH SALAD
WITH MANDARIN ORANGE AND
RED ONIONS

2

ORANGE ROUGHY WITH
SWEET AND HOT PEPPERS AND
MANILA CLAMS

3

ORANGE AND ALMOND COUSCOUS

Whether John and I are together or one of us is away, we both always eat late; nine or ten o'clock is the norm. Because we eat late, we often eat lightly. This entrée of orange roughy and a few manila clams is John's creation. It is a take-off on a Chinese chicken and hot pepper dish he orders from his favorite Chinese restaurant, The Cottage. He uses fish and very little oil for a healthy late-night light-bite. I added a sweet salad to balance the spicy main course and a little couscous to catch all the yummy juices. It makes a great meal for intimate entertaining and it can be easily adapted to serve 2 or 6 people.

BABY SPINACH SALAD
with mandarin orange and red onions

8 ounces (5 to 6 cups) baby spinach

1 cup mandarin oranges, drained

1/2 cup chopped red onions

1 tablespoon orange marmalade

2 tablespoons red wine vinegar

1/3 cup extra-virgin olive oil (evoo) (eyeball it)

Salt and freshly ground black pepper, to taste

Arrange spinach leaves on a large platter or individual salad plates. Top with mandarin sections and chopped red onion. Whisk together marmalade and vinegar. Stream oil into dressing while continuing to whisk.

When you are ready to serve, pour dressing over salad and season with salt and pepper.

ORANGE ROUGHY with sweet
and hot peppers and MANILA CLAMS

4 portions (6 ounces each) orange roughy fillets

Coarse salt and freshly ground black pepper, to taste

3 tablespoons extra-virgin olive oil (evoo)

3 cloves garlic, chopped

1 small to medium yellow onion, sliced

1 red bell pepper, seeded, quartered lengthwise, then sliced into 1/2-inch strips

6 pepperoncini hot peppers, chopped

1/2 pint grape tomatoes

1 cup white wine

20 to 24 manila clams
1/4 cup chopped fresh flat-leaf parsley **(a couple handfuls)**

Season fish with salt and pepper. Heat a large nonstick skillet over medium-high heat. Add 2 tablespoons evoo (twice around the pan). Add fish to pan and cook 2 minutes on each side, carefully transfer to a plate with a thin spatula and loosely cover with foil.

Add another tablespoon evoo (once more around the pan), then add garlic, onions, red bell peppers, and chopped hot peppers. Season veggies with salt and pepper. Sauté 5 minutes, stirring frequently. Add tomatoes and cook a minute more. Deglaze the pan with wine, scraping up the drippings with a wooden spoon. Slide fish back into pan and add manila clams. Cover the pan and reduce heat to simmer. Cook 5 minutes. Sprinkle parsley over the fish and clams and discard any unopened clams. Serve fish and clams on a bed of orange and almond couscous.

orange and almond COUSCOUS

2 ounces (1/4 cup) sliced almonds
1 & 1/2 cups chicken broth
1 tablespoon extra-virgin olive oil **(evoo)**
1 & 1/2 cups plain couscous
Grated zest of 2 navel oranges
2 tablespoons chopped fresh flat-leaf parsley **(a handful)**

Toast nuts in the bottom of a medium saucepan over medium heat. Transfer toasted nuts to a dish and reserve. Return pot to the stovetop. Add broth and evoo, cover pot and raise heat; bring broth to a boil. Remove pot from heat immediately. Add couscous, orange zest, and parsley, then stir. Cover and let couscous stand, 5 minutes. Fluff cooked couscous with a fork and toss with toasted almonds.

TIP
Slice zested oranges and serve them after dinner.

30 MINUTE MEALS

MENU

Serves 4

A GRAND NIGHT IN BERMUDA

1

RED LEAF AND WATERCRESS SALAD
WITH LIME-GINGER DRESSING

2

BAKED SEAFOOD WITH
SHERRY CREAM

3

RICE PILAF WITH PARSLEY
AND SCALLIONS

4

DARK AND STORMY SUNDAES

red leaf and watercress SALAD
with lime-ginger dressing

1 bag (6 ounces) ready-to-use red leaf lettuce, chopped
1 to 1 & 1/2 cups chopped watercress leaves (1 bundle), trimmed
4 radishes, sliced
1/4 English (seedless) cucumber, sliced
3 tablespoons honey
Juice of 1 lime
2 tablespoons white wine vinegar or sherry vinegar
2 inches fresh gingerroot, grated or minced
1/3 cup peanut or vegetable oil
Salt and freshly ground black pepper, to taste

Combine lettuce, watercress, radishes, and cucumbers in a bowl. Whisk together honey, lime juice, vinegar, and ginger. Whisk oil into dressing. Dress salad and toss. Season with salt and pepper, to taste.

BAKED SEAFOOD with sherry cream and RICE PILAF with parsley and scallions

Rice Pilaf

1 box (about 6 ounces) rice pilaf (such as Near East brand)
1 cup chicken broth
2 tablespoons chopped parsley
2 scallions, chopped

Seafood

1 tablespoon extra-virgin olive oil (evoo)
2 tablespoons butter
2 cloves garlic, chopped
2 shallots, chopped
2 stalks celery, from the heart of the stalk, chopped
8 medium white mushrooms, thinly sliced
Coarse Salt and freshly ground black pepper, to taste
1/2 red bell pepper, seeded and chopped
2 tablespoons all-purpose flour

1 & 3/4 cups chicken broth (14-ounce can)

1 cup half-and-half or heavy cream (8 ounce container)

1/4 cup dry sherry (eyeball it)

1 teaspoon cayenne pepper sauce (such as Tabasco) (eyeball it)

1 pound cod, cut into 4-ounce chunks

3/4 pound large shrimp, peeled and deveined (ask for easy-peels at seafood counter of market)

3/4 pound sea scallops, patted dry, foot trimmed if necessary

1/2 cup frozen peas

2 ounces sliced almonds (1/4 cup), for garnish

2 tablespoons chopped fresh flat-leaf parsley, for garnish

Make the rice pilaf: Prepare rice to package directions, using 1 cup chicken broth in place of 1 cup of the water called for. When rice is almost done, 16 minutes, add parsley and scallions to the pot. Remove rice from the heat, fluff with a fork, cover, and let stand until ready to serve.

While the rice is cooking, prepare the seafood: To a large skillet preheated over medium-high heat, add evoo then butter. When the butter has melted into the oil, add garlic, shallots, celery, and mushrooms. Season with salt and pepper. Sauté 4 to 5 minutes, add bell pepper and sauté 2 minutes more. Sprinkle pan with flour and let it cook 1 minute. Whisk in broth and bring the broth to a bubble. Stir in cream, then sherry, then Tabasco. Bring sauce to a bubble. Season seafood with salt and pepper and set cod into simmering sauce. Cook cod about 3 minutes, then slide in shrimp and scallops. When sauce returns to a bubble, cook seafood until scallops are opaque and shrimp tails curl towards head, 4 or 5 minutes. Stir in peas. Thicken sauce one more minute or two and heat peas. Remove pan from stove and serve.

Spoon rice into a shallow bowl or deep plate; top with seafood and sauce. Garnish the seafood with almonds and parsley.

dark and stormy SUNDAES

2 tablespoons butter

3 ripe bananas, **sliced on an angle**

2 tablespoons brown sugar

4 ounces dark rum

Juice of 1 lime

1 pint vanilla bean ice cream

12 ginger snaps, **crumbled**

1 canister real whipped cream

1/2 cup toasted coconut

Maraschino **cherries**

In a medium skillet over medium-high heat, melt butter then add bananas. Sauté bananas 3 minutes, then sprinkle with brown sugar and sauté 2 minutes more. Pull pan off burner and away from the stovetop. Add rum to the pan. Return pan to heat and flame rum. When rum burns out, add lime juice to the pan.

Spoon bananas and sauce into large martini glasses or into dessert cups of your choosing. Top with vanilla bean ice cream, ginger snaps, whipped cream, toasted coconut, and a cherry.

30 MINUTE MEALS

MENU

Serves 4

POSITANO DINNER

1
•

GEMELLI WITH TUNA AND
CHERRY TOMATOES

2
•

COD WITH FENNEL AND ONION

3
•

STRAWBERRIES WITH
SUGAR AND LEMON

My favorite hotel in the entire world, to date, is the San Pietro in Positano, Italy. Not much renders me speechless in this life—the San Pietro does. There are no words to fully describe the beauty of this place, carved into the cliffs, hanging on the flowering, lemon-tree-lined jagged edges of the Amalfi coast, high above the Mediterranean. From the water, the hotel—the entire village for that matter—looks like an enormous tiered wedding cake.

In the village of Positano, at the bottom of the first set of steps to get to the pebbled beach below, is my favorite bistro, Max Bistro. This meal, inspired by the memory of wonderful meals there, allows me to pretend I am in Positano, any night of the week.

COD with fennel and onion

1 large bulb fennel, trimmed of tough tops (2 tablespoons of the fronds reserved for garnish)

2 tablespoons extra-virgin olive oil (evoo)

1 medium to large yellow onion, thinly sliced

Salt and freshly ground black pepper, to taste

1 cup white wine

1 large or 2 medium Russet potatoes, peeled and very thinly sliced

1 cup chicken broth

1 & 1/2 to 1 & 3/4 pounds cod, cut into 4 portions (6 to 8 ounces each)

1/4 cup chopped fresh flat-leaf parsley (a couple handfuls)

Crusty bread, to pass at table

Heat a large, deep, ovenproof skillet over medium-high heat. Preheat oven to 425°F.

Cut tops off the fennel bulb. Reserve a few fronds (lacy, dill-like greens), and chop. Quarter the bulb, then cut into each quarter on an angle to remove the core. Thinly slice the fennel.

Add evoo, fennel, and onion to the pan and sauté them, stirring frequently, 5 minutes. Season with salt. Add wine and reduce by half. Add potatoes to the pan in thin layers, completely covering the fennel and onions, working all the way to the edges of the pan. Pour the broth evenly over the pan. Season fish with salt and pepper. Arrange the fish on the potatoes. Bring the liquids to a bubble. Cover the pan and transfer to oven. Bake fish 15 minutes, until opaque, then uncover and roast 2 or 3 minutes more. Transfer fish and vegetables to shallow bowls or dinner plates and garnish with parsley and fennel fronds. Spoon juices down over the food. Serve with crusty bread for dipping.

GEMELLI with tuna and cherry tomatoes

3 tablespoons extra-virgin olive oil (evoo) (3 times around the pan in a slow stream)

6 cloves garlic, finely chopped

2 cans (6 ounces each) Italian tuna in olive oil, drained

1/2 pint small cherry or grape tomatoes, coarsely chopped

Coarse salt and fresh black pepper, to taste

1 pound gemelli pasta (short braids of pasta, other short-cut pastas can be substituted), cooked to al dente in salted water

1/3 cup chopped fresh flat-leaf parsley (about 3 handfuls)

20 leaves fresh basil, shredded

Heat a large, deep skillet over medium heat. Add evoo and garlic to the pan. When garlic speaks by sizzling in oil, add tuna and mash into oil with the back of a wooden spoon. Let the tuna sit in the oil 5 to 10 minutes to infuse the fish flavor into the evoo and to give the tuna time to break down; it will almost melt into the evoo. Raise the flame a bit and add the coarsely chopped tomatoes to the pan. Season with salt and pepper. Heat the tomatoes through, 2 minutes, then add hot, drained pasta that has been cooked to al dente. Add parsley to the tuna and pasta and toss to combine well and evenly coat pasta. Adjust seasonings. Top pasta with shredded basil and serve.

STRAWBERRIES with sugar and lemon

In Positano, the strawberries are wild, tiny, and so sweet that the locals dress them with Amalfi lemon juice to mellow them. It is the perfect, light dessert. A little Limoncello (lemon liqueur), well chilled, only improves the experience. At home, I look for small strawberries, in season, add a little sugar and lemon, and let the berries sit a while. It's as close as I can get to Max without the plane ticket.

1 pint small strawberries, hulled and halved

2 teaspoons sugar

Juice of 1/2 lemon

Mint sprigs, for garnish

Combine strawberries with sugar and lemon juice and let stand 20 minutes or more. Serve with a few torn leaves of fresh mint.

30
MINUTE
MEALS

MENU

Serves 4

ROAD TO MOROCCO DOUBLE-DATE NIGHT

1

SMOKED ALMOND-STUFFED DATES

2

GREEN PEPPER AND
TOMATO SALAD

3

QUICK TAGINE-STYLE CHICKEN
WITH COUSCOUS

Serve this meal at the coffee table rather than the dining room table. Place throw pillows on the floor around the coffee table for the seating. Light some candles, throw a red scarf over the lamp shade, and play some exotic music to set a real scene—you'll have your guests belly dancing in no time!

smoked almond-stuffed DATES

20 whole smoked almonds
20 whole pitted dates

Cut a slit into each date. Wedge an almond in the date, running lengthwise. Set the nuts into the dates with the nuts resting lengthwise on the dates. Don't wedge the nut in too deeply; it should rest half in and half out of the date. Arrange filled fruit on a small serving plate.

green pepper and tomato SALAD

2 green bell peppers, seeded and cut into 1 & 1/2-inch dice
3 vine-ripe tomatoes, seeded and diced
1 small onion, chopped
1 large clove garlic, finely chopped
1/2 cup fresh flat-leaf parsley leaves, coarsely chopped
Juice of 1/2 lemon (1 tablespoon)
1 tablespoon red wine vinegar
3 tablespoons extra-virgin olive oil (evoo)
Salt and freshly ground black pepper, to taste
1 teaspoon ground cumin (1/2 a palmful)

Combine peppers, tomatoes, onions, garlic, and parsley in a bowl with your fingertips. Squeeze the juice from the lemon with the lemon half sitting upright; the lemon juice will spill down over the sides of the lemon and the seeds will remain with the fruit. Squeeze the juice evenly over the salad. If the lemon is underripe, microwave it for 10 seconds before you cut into it. Next, sprinkle a tablespoon of vinegar over the salad—just eyeball it. Drizzle the evoo over the salad, add salt, pepper, and cumin. Toss again. Taste to adjust seasonings and serve.

TIP
Fill out menu with:

•

Mint tea

•

Fruit cookies
(such as Pepperidge Farm
apricot cookies)

quick tagine-style CHICKEN with couscous

Cubed tender cuts of lamb or diced eggplant or tofu may be substituted for the chicken in this dish.

Chicken

    2 tablespoons extra-virgin olive oil (evoo)

    4 cloves garlic, smashed beneath the flat of your knife with the heel of your hand, skins discarded

    1 & 1/2 to 1 & 3/4 pounds boneless, skinless chicken breasts, cut into large bite-size pieces

    2 medium or 1 large yellow onion, quartered and sliced

    10 pitted prunes, coarsely chopped

    1/4 cup golden raisins (1-ounce box)

    2 cups low-sodium chicken broth (available in paper containers on soup aisle)

    1 tablespoon grill seasoning blend, such as Montreal Seasoning by McCormick, or coarse salt and freshly ground black pepper, to taste

> **TIP**
>
> Double or triple the recipe for spices and store in cool dry place, tightly sealed, for use in future Moroccan-flavored dishes.

Spice blend

1 & 1/2 teaspoons cumin (1/2 palmful)

1 & 1/2 teaspoons sweet paprika (eyeball it)

1/2 teaspoon coriander (eyeball it)

1/2 teaspoon turmeric (eyeball it)

1/8 teaspoon cinnamon (a couple pinches)

Couscous

    1 can (14 ounces) chicken broth (about 2 cups)

    2 cups couscous

    2 tablespoons extra-virgin olive oil (evoo) (eyeball it)

    2 scallions, finely chopped

Condiments

    Mango chutney any variety and brand (available on the condiment or international food aisle)

    Chopped cilantro leaves or fresh flat-leaf parsley

    Finely chopped scallions

Make the chicken: Heat a large nonstick skillet over medium-high heat. Add evoo, twice around the pan in a slow stream, and smashed garlic. Scatter chicken around the pan in an even layer. Cook chicken pieces 2 minutes on each side to brown, then add onions, prunes, raisins, and broth. Mix spices in a small dish and scatter over the pot. Cover and reduce heat to moderate. Cook 7 or 8 minutes; remove the lid and stir.

Prepare the couscous: Bring chicken broth to a boil. Add couscous, evoo, and scallions and remove the couscous from the stove immediately. Cover and let stand 5 minutes. Fluff the couscous with a fork.

Uncover chicken and cook another 2 to 3 minutes to thicken sauce slightly. Adjust the seasoning to taste and serve chicken on a bed of couscous with chopped cilantro and chopped scallions for garnish.

Serves 10

COOKING FOR 10
IN 30
ITALIAN STYLE

1
•

EGGPLANT "CAVIAR"

2
•

TUSCAN-STYLE CHICKEN
WITH ROSEMARY

3
•

WILD MUSHROOM RISOTTO

4
•

MIXED GREENS SALAD

eggplant "CAVIAR"

The seeds of the eggplant look like caviar. In my family, this spread is sometimes called Poor Man's Caviar.

1 medium firm eggplant

1 clove garlic, cracked away from the skin

2 pinches ground allspice

Coarse salt and fresh black pepper, to taste

A handful of fresh flat-leaf parsley leaves

A drizzle of extra-virgin olive oil (evoo)

1 whole-grain baguette or other long crusty bread, sliced at bread counter

Preheat oven to highest setting, 500°F.

Cut 2 or 3 slits into one side of a whole eggplant. Place eggplant directly on the oven rack in the middle of the oven and roast for 20 minutes or until eggplant is tender. Keep the slits facing up so that the eggplant does not lose liquids as it roasts.

The roasted eggplant will look like a flat tire when you remove it from the oven. Using a sharp utility knife, carefully peel skin away from eggplant flesh, discarding skin. Add cooked eggplant flesh and juice to food processor and combine with garlic, allspice, salt, pepper, parsley, and evoo. Pulse-grind the eggplant into a paste and transfer to a serving dish.

To serve, surround a bowlful of spread with crusty bread rounds.

wild mushroom RISOTTO

6 ounces dried porcini mushrooms (found in produce department)

1 quart beef stock

1 quart water

2 tablespoons extra-virgin olive oil (evoo) (twice around the pan)

1 tablespoon butter

2 shallots, finely chopped

2 cups Arborio rice

1/2 cup dry sherry or 1/4 cup cognac

8 sprigs fresh thyme, leaves stripped and chopped (about 3 tablespoons)

3/4 cup Parmigiano Reggiano cheese (eyeball it)

Salt and freshly ground black pepper, to taste

Place dried porcini mushrooms, stock, and water in a saucepan and bring to a boil, then reduce heat to low.

In a large skillet, heat evoo and butter over medium to medium-high heat. Add shallots and sauté 2 minutes. Add Arborio rice and sauté, 2 or 3 minutes more. Add sherry or cognac and cook the liquid completely out. Add several ladles of hot stock or broth and reduce heat slightly. Simmer, stirring frequently until liquid is absorbed.

Remove mushrooms from water and reserve cooking liquid. Coarsely chop the mushrooms and add them to the rice. Continue to ladle broth into rice, stirring mixture each time you add broth. Wait until the liquid is absorbed before adding more broth. When the rice is cooked to al dente, stir in thyme and cheese. Season with salt and pepper, to taste. The ideal total cooking time for perfect risotto is 22 minutes. The consistency should be creamy from the starch of the rice.

tuscan-style CHICKEN with rosemary

2 pounds boneless, skinless chicken thighs
1 & 1/2 pounds chicken tenderloins
Salt **and freshly ground black** pepper**, to taste**
3 tablespoons extra-virgin olive oil **(evoo)**
6 cloves garlic**, crushed**
2 tablespoons white wine vinegar
2 tablespoons butter
2 shallots**, chopped**
6 sprigs fresh rosemary**, leaves stripped and finely chopped**
2 tablespoons all-purpose flour
1 cup dry white wine
2 cups beef broth **(yes, beef broth)**

Heat a large, deep skillet over medium-high heat. Season chicken with salt and pepper. Add 2 tablespoons evoo (twice around the pan), half the chicken pieces, and a couple of cloves of crushed garlic.

Brown chicken 2 minutes on each side and remove from pan. Add the remaining tablespoon evoo (another single turn of the pan), the remaining chicken pieces, and the remaining garlic. Brown chicken 2 minutes on each side and remove. Add 2 tablespoons vinegar to the pan (2 splashes); let it cook off. Add butter, shallots, and rosemary to the pan and cook 2 minutes. Add flour and cook 1 minute more. Whisk in wine; reduce 1 minute. Whisk in broth and bring liquids up to a bubble. Return chicken to the pan and simmer over moderate heat, 7 to 8 minutes to finish cooking chicken through.

mixed greens SALAD

2 sacks ready-to-use mixed greens
3 tablespoons balsamic **vinegar**
1/4 cup extra-virgin olive oil **(evoo)**
Salt **and freshly ground black** pepper**, to taste**
Edible flowers**, for garnish (available in produce department near the herbs)**

Place greens in a large salad bowl. Toss with balsamic vinegar and evoo; season with salt and pepper. Scatter the flowers across salad bowl to garnish.

> **TIP**
>
> Fill out menu with:
>
> •
>
> Italian cheeses and olives
>
> •
>
> Bread sticks
>
> •
>
> For dessert, an Italian cookie or mini-pastry tray (store-bought)

30 MINUTE MEALS

MENU

Serves 8

COOKING FOR 8 IN 30 FRENCH STYLE

1
•

FOOL-YA-BAISE
SEAFOOD STEW

2
•

MIXED GREENS SALAD
WITH LEMON, OLIVES, AND
ANCHOVIES

3
•

EASY LEMON MOUSSE

FOOL-YA-BAISE seafood stew

3 tablespoons extra-virgin olive oil (evoo) (3 times around the pan)

1 teaspoon fennel seed (1/3 palmful)

6 cloves garlic, chopped

1 leek, sliced lengthwise, then across, 1/2-inch slices, then washed

1 medium onion, chopped

2 stalks celery, split lengthwise, then chopped

1 bay leaf

Salt and freshly ground black pepper, to taste

1 small bundle fresh thyme sprigs (4 to 6 sprigs), left whole

2 three-to-four-inch pieces orange peel, made with vegetable peeler

1/2 cup chopped fresh flat-leaf parsley (3 handfuls)

1 cup dry white wine

4 cups chicken broth

1 can (15 ounces) chunky-style crushed or diced tomatoes

3 pounds fish, such as red snapper and tilapia, cut into 2-inch pieces

12 sea scallops, halved

2 baguettes, sliced at the bakery counter

Rouille

4 cloves garlic, cracked away from skin

2 roasted red peppers (jarred is fine but pat them dry)

1/2 teaspoon salt

2 small red chile peppers, seeded, or 1 teaspoon crushed red pepper flakes

6 half-inch slices baguette, crust trimmed

1/4 cup stock from above stew, taken as it cooks

1 cup extra-virgin olive oil (evoo)

Heat a wide, heavy pot over medium-high heat. Add evoo, about 3 tablespoons (3 times around the pan). Add fennel seed, garlic, leeks, onions, celery, and bay. Season with salt and pepper. Add thyme sprigs, orange peels, and 2 handfuls parsley, reserving some chopped parsley for garnish. Stir to combine seasonings with vegetables. Sauté vegetables, 5 to 8 minutes, until leeks are tender but still green. Stir in wine and cook, 1 to 2 minutes. Add chicken broth and tomatoes and stir well to combine. Arrange fish and scallops around the pan. Spoon soup stock over and around

seafood. Season with salt and pepper. Cover pan and cook 10 to 12 minutes, until
fish and scallops are opaque.

Preheat oven to 250°F.

Reserve at least bread 6 slices for rouille. Spread remaining slices on a cookie sheet.
Place sheet in oven to lightly toast sliced bread.

Make the rouille: In a food processor, place garlic, well-drained roasted red peppers, salt,
and the chile peppers. Tear the 6 pieces of bread into pieces and arrange around
the food processor bowl. Steal a ladle of the stock, about 1/4 cup, from fish stew as it
cooks and pour it over the bread to moisten it. Pulse pepper and bread together,
then turn processor on. Stream in about 1 cup evoo in a slow, steady stream. When
mixture is smooth and well combined, transfer to a small serving bowl.

When fish and scallops are cooked through, arrange cooked seafood in shallow bowls.
Stir soup and ladle it and over seafood. While you are serving up stew be on the
lookout for bay leaves, thyme stems, or orange peels and discard as you find them.
Garnish stew with remaining parsley. Serve Fool-ya-baise with toasted bread
rounds, which should be spread with rouille and set afloat on top of bowlfuls of stew.

mixed greens SALAD

with lemon, olives, and anchovies

2 hearts of romaine, **chopped**

1 sack (6 cups) mixed baby greens

Juice of 2 lemons

Salt **and freshly ground black** pepper, **to taste**

1/3 cup extra-virgin olive oil **(evoo), enough to coat greens evenly**

1 cup pitted fancy black or green olives **(from specialty olive case near
deli counter)**

1 tin flat anchovies **fillets, drained**

1/4 cup chopped or snipped fresh chives

Toss greens with lemon juice, salt, and pepper. Coat greens with evoo and toss them
again. Add olives and arrange anchovies around the salad bowl. Sprinkle with
chopped chives.

easy lemon MOUSSE

2 packages lemon instant pudding

Milk **(amount depends on pudding brand, check panel on box)**

2 cups whipped cream **or whipped topping (store-bought)**

1/2 pint raspberries, **for garnish**

Butter cookies **or shortbread rounds**

In a medium bowl, stir together pudding and milk and set aside. Fold whipped cream into pudding and serve in small bowls or cocktail glasses garnished with raspberries. Place dessert glasses on a dessert plate. Arrange cookies alongside the mousse.

DINNER AT 8 BETTER THAN A RESTAURANT 24/7

30 MINUTE MEALS

MENU

Serves 6

LINGER AT THE TABLE, NOT AT THE STOVE

1
•

SWISS AND BACON DIP

2
•

CHICKEN WITH RED WINE
AND TARRAGON

swiss and bacon DIP

8 slices center-cut bacon, chopped

8 ounces cream cheese, softened

1/2 cup mayonnaise

2 rounded teaspoons Dijon mustard

1 & 1/2 cups shredded Swiss cheese (available preshredded on dairy aisle)

3 scallions, chopped

1/2 cup smoked almonds, coarsely chopped

Baby carrots, for dipping

Selection of spiced flat breads, cocktail-size pumpernickel or rye breads, or sliced whole-grain baguettes, for dipping

Preheat oven to 400°F.

Brown bacon in a nonstick skillet over medium-high heat. Drain crisp bacon bits on paper towels.

In a mixing bowl, combine cream cheese, mayonnaise, Dijon, Swiss cheese, and scallions with cooked bacon. Transfer to a shallow small casserole or baking dish and bake until golden and bubbly at edges, 15 to 18 minutes. Top with chopped smoked almonds. Place dip on a platter and surround warm casserole with carrots and breads for dipping.

> **TIP**
>
> Variation:
>
> •
>
> **S&B Dip with Horseradish**
>
> •
>
> Stir in 2 rounded teaspoons prepared horseradish when combining cheese and bacon.

CHICKEN with red wine and tarragon

- 2 tablespoons extra-virgin olive oil (evoo) (twice around the pan in a slow stream)
- 2 & 1/4 pounds boneless skinless chicken breast, thighs, or combination of both, cut into chunks
- Coarse salt and freshly ground black pepper, to taste
- 2 tablespoons butter
- 2 shallots, chopped
- 1 carrot, chopped into fine dice
- 1 rounded teaspoon sugar
- 12 crimini (baby portobello) mushrooms, sliced or chopped
- 4 to 5 sprigs fresh tarragon, leaves stripped and chopped (about 2 tablespoons)
- A handful of fresh flat-leaf parsley leaves, chopped
- 1 & 1/3 cups good dry red wine, such as Burgundy (eyeball it) (about 1/4 bottle)
- 1 can (15 ounces) chunky-style crushed tomatoes or diced tomatoes in puree

Noodles

- 3/4 pound extra-wide egg noodles, cooked until just tender, about 6 minutes
- 2 tablespoons butter, cut into bits
- 2 sprigs fresh tarragon, leaves stripped and chopped (about 1 tablespoon)
- A handful of fresh flat-leaf parsley leaves, chopped (about 2 tablespoons)

In a large skillet over medium-high heat brown pieces of chicken in evoo for 2 or 3 minutes on each side and remove to a plate.

Return pan to stove and reduce heat to medium. Add butter to the pan then shallots, carrots, and mushrooms. Sauté 3 to 5 minutes until mushrooms darken and carrot bits are fork-tender. Add sugar, tarragon, and parsley and stir. Add wine and reduce liquid for 2 minutes. Add tomatoes to sauce and stir to combine. Add chicken back to the pan and simmer chicken in sauce for 6 minutes or until chicken is cooked through and juices run clear.

Place cooked egg noodles in a serving dish and toss with butter and herbs; serve chicken alongside.

Serves 6

FAST, SLOW-COOKING DINNER

1

SUNDAY GRAVY AND MACARONI

2

ROMAINE HEARTS WITH ROASTED RED PEPPER VINAIGRETTE

On Sundays, my Grandpa Emmanuel would take the kitchen table out on the lawn and turn it into a buffet table for his 10 children and the whole neighborhood. He would make Sunday gravy (marinara sauce) filled with slow-cooked meats that flavored the sauce: braciole, pork chops, chicken thighs, rabbit, sausages, and meatballs. He would simmer the meats for hours, then pull them from the saucepan and separate them into stacks on a large platter. He would toss spaghetti, which he referred to as "macaroni" in English, with some of the sauce and add lots of cheese to it. If you had any room left for dessert, he'd split open one of his own hand melons, in season, scoop the seeds out with his bare hand and fill the melon with vanilla ice cream. Not a bad idea at all—if you have the room!

SUNDAY GRAVY and macaroni

This recipe for gravy and macaroni is the best I can do in 30 minutes to bring back Sundays with Emmanuel. Enjoy it any night you choose.

1 pound spaghetti

Salt and freshly ground black pepper, to taste

3 thin-cut (1/2-inch-thick) pork loin chops

2 sweet Italian sausage links

2 hot Italian sausage links

1/4 cup extra-virgin olive oil (evoo)

5 cloves garlic

1/2 to 1 teaspoon crushed red pepper flakes, for moderate to spicy marinara

1 cup beef broth

1 can (28 ounces) crushed tomatoes

1 can (14 ounces) diced tomatoes

1/4 cup chopped fresh flat-leaf parsley (a couple handfuls of leaves)

Several leaves fresh basil, torn or chopped (a handful)

1 pound meatloaf mix (ground beef, pork, and veal combined)

1 egg

1 small onion, minced

1/3 cup grated Parmigiano Reggiano cheese (2 handfuls), plus more for tossing with pasta and to pass at table

1/2 cup Italian bread crumbs (3 handfuls)

Crusty bread, to pass at table

Bring a large pot of water to a boil. Salt water and cook pasta 7 to 8 minutes, to al dente. Drain.

Preheat oven to 425°F.

Heat a deep skillet or medium heavy-bottomed saucepan over medium-high heat. Season pork chops with salt and pepper. Cut sausages in half. Add 1 tablespoon evoo (once around the pan) to pan. Place chops in pan and brown 2 minutes on each side, remove. Add another tablespoon evoo and sausages. Brown sausages 2 minutes on each side and transfer to plate with pork. Add 3 cloves chopped garlic and crushed red pepper flakes to the pot and sauté, 1 minute. Add beef broth to the pan and scrape up drippings. Add tomatoes and herbs and bring sauce to a bubble. Add meats back to the pot and reduce heat to simmer. Simmer sauce until ready to serve, 12 to 15 minutes.

Make the meatballs: Combine ground meat, egg, onion, the remaining 2 cloves chopped garlic, 1/3 cup cheese, and the bread crumbs. Season with salt and pepper and roll balls, 1 & 1/2 to 2 inches in size. Place balls on a nonstick cookie sheet. Roast meatballs 10 minutes, then slide into Sunday sauce and turn off oven. Add bread to oven to crisp crust.

To serve, place pork, sausages, and meatballs on a serving dish. Pour half of the sauce into a separate serving dish to ladle over pasta and meats at the table. Toss cooked spaghetti with remaining sauce in saucepan, adding a few handfuls of grated cheese as you toss it. Transfer pasta to a serving dish. Pass additional cheese at the table.

ROMAINE HEARTS
with roasted red pepper vinaigrette

3 hearts of romaine, chopped

1 roasted red pepper, drained

2 tablespoons red wine vinegar (eyeball it)

A handful of fresh flat-leaf parsley

1/3 cup extra-virgin olive oil (evoo) (eyeball it)

Salt and freshly ground black pepper, to taste

Place chopped romaine on a platter or in a salad bowl. To a food processor, add roasted red pepper, vinegar, and parsley. Process, then stream in evoo. Season with salt and pepper. Remove processor bowl and drizzle dressing over salad; serve.

30 MINUTE MEALS

MENU

Serves 4

GERMAN HEIRLOOM

1
●

ANNA MARIA'S
ROULADEN

2
●

SAUTÉED RED CABBAGE

3
●

GINGER-LEMON
DESSERT CUPS

anna maria's ROULADEN

My friend Anna Maria was born in Germany and makes a simple and simply delicious rouladen. I told her I wanted to make it into a 30-minute meal. She said "Good luck!" By using thin-cut sirloin rather than slow-cooking meats, I think this recipe comes close. There is no substitute for Anna Maria's, but if you don't know her, try this out.

Potatoes

2 pounds small potatoes (such as red-skin new potatoes)

2 tablespoons butter

2 tablespoons chopped fresh flat-leaf parsley

Rouladen

4 slices bacon

4 thin slices beef sirloin (just over 1 pound) (ask the butcher to cut the meat 1/4 inch thick)

Salt and freshly ground black pepper, to taste

4 rounded teaspoons Dijon mustard

1 small, yellow onion, finely chopped (1/2 cup)

4 tablespoons chopped fresh flat-leaf parsley (a couple handfuls)

4 dill pickle spears

Toothpicks or kitchen twine

2 tablespoons extra-virgin olive oil (evoo) (twice around the pan)

2 tablespoons butter, cut into pieces

2 tablespoons all-purpose flour

3 cups chicken broth (available on the soup aisle)

1/4 cup sour cream

Boil potatoes in salted water for 8 to 12 minutes, until fork-tender. Drain and coat potatoes in butter and parsley. Keep covered and warm until ready to serve.

Make the rouladen: Place slices of bacon in a skillet over medium heat and render fat by cooking bacon about 3 minutes. As edges just begin to crisp, remove bacon from the skillet and transfer to paper towels to drain.

Season sirloin with salt and pepper. Spread each slice with a rounded spoonful of mustard. Top mustard with chopped onion and a generous scatter of chopped parsley. Top each slice with a slice of bacon and a dill pickle spear. Place the bacon and pickle off-center, closer to one edge of the meat than the other. Roll the steaks around the filling and secure with toothpicks or kitchen twine. Heat a deep skillet over medium-high heat. Add evoo, twice around the pan, then meat rolls. Cook meat 2 to 3 minutes, then give it a quarter turn. Cook meat a total of 10 to 12 minutes, then transfer to a plate. Add butter to the skillet and melt. Add flour to the butter and whisk together, cooking 2 minutes. Add chicken broth to the flour and butter and scrape up pan drippings. Season with salt and pepper. Stir in sour cream and remove from heat.

Remove toothpicks or twine from meat. Set meat roll and potatoes on a dinner plate and cover with sour cream gravy.

sautéed RED CABBAGE

2 tablespoons extra-virgin olive oil **(evoo)**
1 small onion, **sliced**
1/2 red cabbage, **shredded**
1/3 cup white or apple cider vinegar **(eyeball it)**
2 rounded tablespoons sugar
1 teaspoon mustard seeds
Salt **and freshly ground black** pepper, **to taste**

Heat a skillet over medium-high heat. Add evoo and onion and sauté, 2 minutes. Add cabbage and turn in pan, sautéing it until it wilts, 3 to 5 minutes. Add vinegar to the pan and turn the cabbage in it. Sprinkle sugar over the cabbage and turn again. Season with mustard seeds, salt, and pepper and reduce heat a bit. Let cabbage continue to cook, 10 minutes or until ready to serve, stirring occasionally.

ginger-lemon DESSERT CUPS

1 box instant lemon pudding

Cold milk**, amount depends on brand of pudding (check package directions)**

20 to 24 ginger snap cookies

3 tablespoons butter**, melted**

1/2 pint strawberries**, hulled and sliced**

2 pieces crystallized ginger**, finely chopped, for garnish**

Store-bought real whipped cream **in a spray can (from dairy aisle of market)**

Grated zest of 1 lemon

Mix pudding with milk to package directions and let stand 5 minutes. Grind ginger snaps in a food processor into crumbs. Remove bowl from processor and take out blade. Add butter to the food processor and stir to moisten the crumbs. Pour crumbs into 4 small glass bowls and press the crumbs up the sides of the bowls, lining each dish with a ginger snap "crust." Add a few slices of strawberries to each bowl. Fill each dish with lemon pudding and top with a few more sliced berries and chopped crystallized ginger. Add a whipped cream rosette to each dessert and garnish with lemon zest.

INDEX